CJ00797199

THE FIRST SLAP

A Woman's Journey From Domestic Abuse
Expertly Uncovered

AUTHORED BY TARA K.
EXPERT CO-AUTHORS:
DR RAVJOT KAUR & HARPAL S. CHATWAL

Disclaimer

This book is designed to provide information and motivation to our readers. It is sold with the understanding that the author and publisher are not engaged to render any type of psychological, legal, or any other kind of professional advice. The content is the sole expression and opinion of its author. Neither the publisher nor the individual author(s) shall be liable for any physical, psychological, emotional, financial, or commercial damages, including, but not limited to, special, incidental, consequential or other damages. Our views and rights are the same: You are responsible for your own choices, actions, and results.

The content of the book is solely written by the author.

DVG STAR Publishing are not liable for the content of the book.

Published by DVG STAR PUBLISHING

www.dvgstar.com

email us at info@dvgstar.com

NO PART OF THIS WORK MAY BE REPRODUCED OR STORED IN AN INFORMATIONAL RETRIEVAL SYSTEM, WITHOUT THE EXPRESS PERMISSION OF THE PUBLISHER IN WRITING.

Copyright © 2019 Tara K., Dr Ravjot Kaur & Harpal S. Chatwal

All rights reserved.

ISBN: 1-912547-29-5
ISBN-13: 978-1-912547-29-6

DEDICATION

To our loved ones, especially our mothers.

.

FOREWORD

Domestic violence also known as domestic abuse is a significant social and public health issue affecting a substantial proportion of families in the United Kingdom. The impact of domestic violence and abuse can be devastating. In the worst instances, it results in serious injury or even death.

A couple of decades ago domestic abuse victims were often terrified and ashamed of coming forward to tell their stories. They were worried that they would be either blamed for their abuse or rejected by their community for voicing their concerns. Some cultures used to argue that gender roles, a fixation on control, and a culture of aggression have ingrained domestic violence into the way of life and were unaware of the long term implications for the health and wellbeing of victims, including poor physical and mental health conditions, isolation and often substance misuse.

Children and young people suffer too as a result of such violence and abuse. There is a significant risk to the child's physical, emotional and social development and an increased risk they themselves will become victims of abuse themselves, or even perpetrators. In the United Kingdom according to the latest statistical data from the Local Government Association, domestic abuse accounts for eight percent of all crime with an estimated two million victims a year. Victims are predominantly women, with one in four women experiencing a form of domestic abuse in their lifetime. Although domestic violence campaigns often focus on women, both men and women can be and are victims of domestic abuse.

Violence survivors are often asked why they don't leave. But consider this, how would you feel about leaving your partner? As difficult as it may be to admit, domestic violence relationships still offer their victims something, such as financial security or a relationship with the person they love. Perhaps most important, though, is the fact that leaving can be dangerous and may have a significant financial impact on personal life or on their children's life, therefore, it's easy to understand why so many survivors are hesitant to leave especially if you have children with your abusive partner.

This book is unique in that it is based on a real life story and after each chapter; the professional authors have given an expert understanding on the main authors' experience. I call this book a special addition and a must have for all professionals and non-professionals dealing with and supporting victims of domestic violence. This book will not only contribute to our knowledge but also contribute to understanding of this issue from a diverse range in a unique approach. As a practicing psychiatrist, I highly recommend this book to my clinical colleagues who are busy supporting domestic abuse victims on a daily basis.

Dr Tariq Khan
Consultant Psychiatrist

The author's vision from the onset was to help others by raising awareness, and assist to create a movement against domestic violence; sharing being an essential part of this, a dedicated website – **www.thefirstslap.com** has been created.

On this website there is a forum where readers can voice their experiences and share their stories with each other.

You are welcome to contact the authors via email – **tara@thefirstslap.com**; they will provide a timely reply and support where needed.

CONTENTS

ACKNOWLEDGMENTS

We are very grateful to a number of people who helped and supported us throughout this journey.

First and foremost, we want to thank the Creator of the universe who has brought the three of us together in order to help others in need.

We wish to acknowledge every person, male or female, adult or child impacted by domestic violence and hope this book will allow you to seek the support you need.

A sincere thanks to John Banks, Anil Rathore, Anil Mehra, Sanjiv Kumar, Fouzia Darr, Richard Stephens, Tarek Hayat, Sandeeren Cunjamalay, Dr Malkit Singh Deogan, Philip Chan, Alamara Awan, Rani Malik, Caroline Makaka, Dr Pauline Long, Jossine Abrahams, Pamela Blackman, Hardeep Bedi, Jodie Green- Phylis, Dav Panesar, Raman Kaur, Joanna Scott, Jatinder Kaur (Australia), Dr Gurprit Pannu, Dr Tariq Khan and Sandeep Kaur.

A special thanks to our respective places of work, members of our community, The Sikh PA, Sangat TV channel, Basic of Sikhi team, EACH, Pukaar and BBC Asian Network.

A big thank you to our siblings, Rajinder, Manjit, Harpreet & Ishbir Rakhra, Kan Singh and Manpal Singh Shah. Of course the rest of our friends and families, especially Jagjit Singh Bajwa who has been our anchor for the past few months!

Lastly a special shout to Mayooran, Labosshy and all of the DVG Star team!

.

CHAPTER 1
NEW BEGINNINGS

And so it begins...

My heart stopped and my eyes glazed over. I stood frozen, as disbelief flooded through me.

It felt as though I wouldn't breathe again, like the life I had was stolen from me. Yet in reality I knew I would live to suffer this pain for another day. My skin on fire, I turn to look at Jas. Time stood still, and I was waiting for something to give.

"You dare not to hug my aunty!"

His stern voice brought me hurtling back to my senses. As my eyes focused on him, I saw the veins pulsing in his neck; I shrank back, waiting for him to explode again. I had no idea what would happen next. He looked at me as though I had stolen from him. I felt so ashamed. His lips curled into a sneer and the disgust was etched into his contorted facial features. I felt terrified. He paced up and down the living room, the look in his eyes alarming me. Clenching his fists and sarcastically laughing, I stood as still as I could, making sure not to make eye contact with him. I was helpless and his intense irritation and resentment astonished me.

I could hear soft muttering in the background; the voice of my mother-in-law talking about me. What had I done wrong? This new family felt like strangers to me. I ran to the bathroom and I could feel their accusing stares, their anger and rage directed at me for a crime I had no idea about!

My mother-in-law was embarrassing me further by telling everyone,

"She should have hugged her aunty, how dare she... silly London girl."

I felt so unsafe in this unpredictable environment. These people are meant to be my new loving family. I looked around at the pictures on the wall; pictures of what I believed to be a kind, respectable family smiling at me. It made my blood run cold. My tea was lukewarm on the side table, and the heating was on full blast; making my face flush, as the stinging intensified.

Three weeks ago, I had been a bride filled with hopes and dreams, ready for a life of joy with my dearest husband, Jas. Now as I looked into the mirror, my reflection told a different story. A livid bruise was appearing on my bright red cheek. My eyes were blood shot from tears and as I raised my hands to softly touch my skin, they started to shake. Feelings of shame crept through me and a wave of tears spilled from my eyes. I couldn't believe that no one cared about my suffering. Who were these people on the other side of the door?

Jas had rushed towards me as I was sitting down in the living room, violently pulling me to a standing position. He then pushed me against the wall, and as the back of my head hit off it, he slapped me hard across my right cheek, with the full force of his hand. The pain was instant, shocking me like nothing has ever done before. I felt unsafe.

A sharp knock at the door made me gasp. Without

consent, my mother-in-law stormed into the bathroom, the fury in her eyes piercing me.

"How dare you? You have brought shame on us."

I tried to remember what I had done, tried to bring back the memories of that day.

That morning, I had visited the Gurdwara (Sikh place of worship). I had spent hours making myself look beautiful, knowing that as a new bride, it would be expected of me. My peach and gold saree shimmered and after hours of preparation, my hair and nails were perfect, and I was excited for the day ahead. I imagined exchanging warm smiles with all the guests and giving them a good lasting impression of my gentleness and kindness as the new daughter-in-law.

At the Gurdwara I was being greeted by so many people, my cheeks ached from the smiling. I felt like I had said the Punjabi way of greeting "Sat Sri Akaal" a thousand times. An older lady smiled at me and came over; she seemed really pleased to see me. We greeted each other again with "Sat Sri Akaal'. She looked at me strangely as she walked away and I caught the eye of my husband, his jaw tense and narrowed, I didn't remember seeing that before. Suddenly, my loving feelings evaporated, and I was left standing alone, unsure of what just happened. I was very uncomfortable and my heart sank into my stomach and gave me such an intense feeling of anxiety, I wanted to escape, and managed to get myself into the ladies toilet and locked myself in a cubicle to compose myself.

What I didn't know was that this was my husband's great aunt. I should have taken her into my arms with a warm embrace. And that was the terrible and horrific crime I had committed in those very few seconds. I had grown up in London and it was outside of what I knew to greet people in any other way than Sat Sri Akaal. I had never before greeted a complete stranger with a hug. How was I to know? And how could this small mistake lead to being slapped?

Only hours ago, I was floating on top of the world with joy in my heart. Now, these feelings had been ripped from my heart. I felt like I had been caught up in a hurricane and left feeling dazed and confused. I could not believe that my husband, the man who was supposed to offer safety and protection had raised his hand to me, left me hurt and raw for a simple error.

This woman, his aunty, was not even a blood relative, yet he had put her feelings before mine; his wife. I was not even given a chance to apologise or explain. I felt despair and helplessness wash over me. In a single second, everything had drastically changed. My whole life seemed to be crumbling beneath me.

During our engagement, I had shared my deepest secrets with Jas. I had bared my soul to him; told him about the violence my mother had endured at home and the effects it had on our family. I confided in him that this was my deepest fear to go through the same pain and suffering as my mother. He was struck with horror, exclaimed that the men who abuse women did not deserve to live. He also mentioned that if anyone did that to his sister, he would "sort them out". He promised me that he would never raise a hand to me, promised that he would fill my life with warmth and love, promised that he would honour me as his wife. I could not accept that this loving man, the man who said he would kill anyone who hurt me, had injured me and shamed me, had looked at me with utter loathing, had left me with a fear I had never before experienced. How could this be?

After I had been given some time to calm myself, I was invited into the lounge for a family conference. As I entered the room, it was as though I was a defendant walking into a trial. The lounge felt like a courtroom; my elder mother-in-law was the judge and the rest of the family were the jury. I was once again reprimanded for acting inappropriately. The sense of injustice surged through me once again. Why was no one mentioning the violent actions of my husband? I looked around at the faces of my supposed family members, all looking at me like I was some sort of a criminal. My face was frozen in an expression of deep shock.

"*These London girls are such cold hearted creatures, did her mother not teach her anything?*"

I heard someone mutter. Tears threatened to spill from my eyes again and all I wanted to do was escape this situation and go back home. I would never be good enough now.

I mentioned "elder mother-in-law" earlier. I had two mother-in-laws. I am not a judgemental person and I accepted the differences in our families but I couldn't ignore the fact that my father-in-law was married to two women. His first wife was unable to have children for many years, so he married his first wife's cousin, someone very closely related to his first wife. Was this normal?

Now living in the North, within a tight knit, highly respectable Asian community, where even strangers would greet each other with warm hugs and no one told me? It just didn't happen where I came from. London life is very different; it's a multicultural cosmopolitan city. People are always on the move. At most people will say "Hello" otherwise I have never really stood still and hugged someone. It would have been nice for someone, anyone to inform me of the local etiquette. I would have been happy to do so. As a qualified social worker, I fully respected the variety of cultural norms and I looked forward to building a loving community of family and friends. I had lots of love and affection to give. I just didn't get the opportunity in London. I wasn't a cold, heartless woman and my mother gave me a lot of advice before I left her home at the tender age of 24. I was just waiting to show them.

I felt very much alone. My own family and close friends were miles away from me and I was surprised and overwhelmed. Did he want to place a boundary in front of everyone to show me what was acceptable and not acceptable? It seemed like a slap was a more appropriate way of dealing with my so-called delinquency. The injustice of it was initially infuriating, I felt like I was screaming into an abyss, but no sound was coming out, no one could hear me. Then I felt a confusion and sadness. Not one of my in-laws said that Jas's behaviour was inappropriate, and that he should never have hit me regardless of what I had or had not done. They gave me the impression that this was my punishment. I was trapped and I couldn't tell anyone, yet.

I kept thinking and asking myself questions. Did I miss something? Did Jas want to marry me? Did his family actually ever like me? Were they ready to accept me as their daughter-in-law? I was beginning to blame myself of choosing him as my future husband.

Jas and I dated for a year before we tied the knot in August 1997. As soon as my friends and families knew that I was coming to the end of my studies, the matchmaking world opened. This was common in our community. Marriage was important for an Indian girl and the ideal age for marriage was before 25, otherwise you were considered to be left on the shelf. I felt the indirect pressure of spending the rest of my life with someone else but I was excited at the same time to experience marriage. We were introduced through a mutual friend; his cousin knew my old school friend and I was a suitable match. Our relationship was long distance but it hardly felt like that. I longed to hear his voice from his daily calls where we would talk for hours, getting to know each other. I was attracted to the way he spoke to me, how his view was of the future and what he wanted for us both.

I could see it, the vision of being in love and becoming married, sharing my deepest thoughts, dreams and feelings with someone. I felt lucky to have found someone who listened to me and it felt like he understood me. I wanted to understand him and bring out the best in him.

Jas was not the first potential partner I met. Our family would often meet other families in London with a son who was ripe and ready for marriage but I always felt rushed as they needed a quick "Yes or No". That was hard to deal with, as I would often think about where I would start work at the same time.

However this introduction did not involve my mother at all. It was our little secret to begin with and I had the luxury of talking to Jas for a few months, before we finally met. It felt like I was making the right decision. He would say all the things I wanted to hear at the right times. He seemed so emotionally intelligent and compassionate; my dream man.

I knew that he had completed his degree a year before and was happy that I met someone who was at a similar stage of life that I was in. He said he was working in his family grocery shop for just a short time while he was looking for the right job he aspired.

I was at the end of finishing my social work degree and was aware that in the North of the country, Child Protection Social Workers, worked directly with children and were given more exposure. This was great for me because in London I felt that if I had stayed I would not be able to develop my experience as much. This really appealed to me at that stage of my career. I felt confident and I was ready to make an impact in children and their families lives.

Near the same time, I was invited to visit my future home and meet my would-be in-laws. As I drove up, the area was like a breath of fresh air. It was open, green and I felt relaxed. I looked around and began to imagine myself here. It was much more peaceful and calmer than London and was shown around the better parts of their city by Jas's family. I couldn't believe that there was hardly any traffic on the roads and all I could see was beautiful views across the countryside. I looked forward to going on romantic walks together. What a perfect place to start my married life, I thought. Jas's family were lovely to me and could not have been nicer. During those months I went to visit a few times, getting used to the area. I wanted to be sure that I could make this my home and it felt like I could.

One afternoon, after a drive with my future in-laws, I sat down for a cup of Indian masala chai with the eldest mother-in-law, Vadhi ma. She shared her life story with me about how she had toughened up, placed a stone on her heart and accepted the reality that her husband would marry her own cousin, as she was not able to conceive. I couldn't believe that she was so open. I heard about how some mother-in-laws can be but I felt touched by her story and I tried to put myself in her shoes. I could imagine the pain and emptiness that she must have felt to not be able to bear a child for the man she loved. Only then to spend so many years watching another woman giving him what he wanted. She didn't have to tell me this. What a genuine person and I felt that I could empathise with her. What a courageous woman, what a tough experience that she has managed to make the best of. I was ready to love her as my own mother.

Vadhi ma said that in her earlier days if women could not have children, her in-laws family would disown her and she was at risk of her husband divorcing her. How horrible would that be to deal with? I felt really sad for her. No one thought about her emotional wellbeing and whom she could share herself with. Vadhi ma's family came up with the idea for her husband to marry within that same family, so she could also remain with her husband. I was taken back when she told me that the sexual side of their relationship had stopped when he married again. I didn't know what to say. She explained that for her, the children born from the second marriage and their happiness had been her only priority all these years. I wanted to give her a hug and acknowledge her sacrifice but I held back not knowing what was appropriate. She had devoted her life to Jas and his sister, Davleena. She said she only wished that Jas were to marry an attractive and intelligent girl and they approved of me very quickly. It felt amazing to be accepted so warmly into the family. Now I felt honoured to be a part of their family and I was so excited for how our lives would be together.

Involving my own mother at this time was too much for me to deal with. Not that she was difficult in any way, she was more protective and I knew she would only want the best for me. She had encouraged and trusted me to get to know Jas better on my own anyway. However she did let me know that she didn't regard him as attractive at all but in the same breath she said, ***"You never know he might be a nice person on the inside!"*** I wasn't sure what to make of that statement from mother and I explained to her that he had qualities that I wanted in a husband. I guess my mother intuitively sensed something about him that she didn't like. You know what a mother's intuition is like right? She didn't want to get in the way of my happiness, but I could tell deep down that she thought he wasn't for me. Typical me, I went ahead with the confidence that I knew best for me. I could feel my mother's concern and her anticipation but I didn't tell her.

I reassured my mother that they were a good, respectable

and honest family. Over the months of talking to him I told my mother he had been nothing but nice and charming to me. He empathised that my parents' marriage had ended and that my mother had brought me up as a single parent. My mother was concerned that I would have two mother-in-laws and was not happy about the situation. She expressed that it was very odd; we just did not hear of this happening before and really wondered and questioned the dynamics of the household. I stuck up for my would-be in-laws and I asked her to keep an open mind. I convinced her repeatedly that I knew they were lovely people living with tragic circumstances. What could she say?

Sooner than I thought, my would-be mother-in-laws had won her over. They told my mother that they would treat me like their daughter and I would have the support of not one but two loving women throughout my life and they would never let me feel like I'm far away from my mother. I felt very much supported simply hearing them tell my mother. She could now be reassured for herself. I would be guided by two powerful supportive women. They also told my mother that because they only had one son at home as their daughter was already married and living down South, so I would be very well cared for. **"From today, she will not be our daughter-in-law, she is more than that, she is our daughter."** I smiled and felt like my family was about to grow. I could let my guards down and I felt they did the right thing by telling my mother with their own voices so that she could hear the reassurance she needed. Very considerately, they even said that they would not take a dowry from my mother and the wedding could be plain and simple. This was yet again another relief to my mother, Indian weddings can become excessively complicated and we were a fairly simple family. I could tell she felt honoured. She smiled. There was no need to be worried from now.

On my wedding day, my mother did everything within her

means to make this a memorable wedding. I felt the pain she felt of letting her daughter, whom she gave birth to, go and start a family of her own. She was very emotional and that in turn made me cry, as I finally understood a deeper layer of the relationship between a mother and daughter. However, closer to the wedding date, when everything was booked, my mother-in-laws both started making more expensive demands from my mother, which was not within her budget and against her faith. I wonder now why they were pushing their weight around. Did we do something or say something wrong? From a religious perspective, we made it clear that we would not be providing meat and alcohol at the wedding. Originally they stated not providing alcohol and meat was fine, but weeks before the wedding they said it was necessary, as their side of the family would not attend a reception party with no alcohol or meat. Wisely, my mother did also end up providing a dowry, as she could see my in-laws would have expectations. To date, I cannot recall what my mother provided in detail, but I know she had a huge heart and she gave my in-laws gold jewellery (as expected) and many expensive items for the whole family. She wisely knew that it was important to give more to the boy's family, as well as giving away her most precious item, her daughter, plus sending her daughter with plenty of sarees and jewellery for her to wear. She was proud of this and held her head high. She knew she did a good job of it. I was oblivious to all of the cultural expectations at the time. I didn't think it was all that important.

I suppose in hindsight, I did not want to disclose and hurt my mother by telling her what kind of people Jas's family had turned out to be. I did not want to admit that she was right because I prayed so much that they would be everything I ever wanted to complete my understanding of what a family should be. She did her very best for me and I wished that she should not have to worry about me any longer. She had lived such a hard life of sacrifice and the only thing she wanted was for her children to be safe and happy. How could I tell her that I apparently dishonoured the family, got slapped by my husband, belittled by my mother-in-laws, who also questioned your parenting skills and that I wanted to run. Hide. Escape. Come back home. I knew she would sit up at night, wonder where she went wrong, wonder what I was going through every second of the day and I honestly did not want to put that on her. I felt so bad that I was harbouring this shameful dangerous secret. It really impacted on my mental health day to day. I didn't know it yet but I started to develop anxiety and I began to become more withdrawn at work.

After the first slap, my emotional state towards Jas dramatically changed. I couldn't help it. I couldn't feel or get close to him anymore. Every touch felt like a deception. The hand that caressed me was also the hand that viciously hit me. The more distance we had the more I began to remember all the things that he had done in the past, and how they were red flags, waiting to develop into something more.

I remembered how he had acted during our honeymoon. He acted so inconsiderately towards me, his dominant uncalled for behaviour left a sour taste in my mouth.

The first morning Jas became upset with me, as I would not eat breakfast. He shouted at me forcing me to eat. I did explain to him that for years I could never stomach breakfast in the morning as it made me feel ill. So my natural morning routine was not to eat anything, or occasionally have a small piece of fruit until lunchtime. Jas would tell me that he knew best and that I should listen to him. Where did all the understanding he had go?

He would go into a mood, like a stroppy teenager, if I would not eat. Firstly I thought he might simply be concerned about my welfare, but I soon became aware that that was not the case in the slightest. He would make me feel guilty for having a bigger lunch and tell me that if I listened to him and ate more at breakfast I would not be eating like a horse at lunchtime. I felt like he was teasing me at first but the words became more offensive each day. When my natural appetite would kick in, Jas would be adamant that I had to wait until he was hungry to eat. His behaviour was so cruel and self-centered. He was being unreasonable.

He had a problem with my freedom of thought, he wanted to control me, he wanted to tell me what he thought was right and wrong and for me to completely submit to that. I can see this now.

I should have recognised it then; that he was extremely oppressive. At the time I just wanted us to have a lovely romantic honeymoon. We had some nice moments, but the food controlling issue left me feeling really unsettled, and it became an issue every day we were away. Thank God our honeymoon was only a long weekend, as we were expected to return for the wedding party for guests who could not attend the wedding. The tradition in those days was that the groom's family would throw a party after the wedding. The honeymoon was not the happy experience I had imagined it to be, it was actually really disappointing, and was clearly an indicator of what was to come. There was an awkward tension between Jas and I at the party. I felt self-conscious about it because other people could see it but the pride in me didn't want people to see it let alone think we weren't getting along.

In our community, especially with the women, there is always this pressure to act very dignified; something that was very hard to do with such strong feelings of anger pushing through me. I didn't want people to talk or for there to be any scandal.

Soon after that, I felt quite silly and let go of the

resentment on my side, I knew that I needed to take hold of the situation and be as mature as I could be, at the time I felt like this was a natural part of marriage, and I prided myself on my ability to help him calm his moods down. So, I started off with an apology. I apologised for not being a breakfast person whilst on our honeymoon and afterwards, I told him I would try and change so that we could eat breakfast together but I also made my views crystal clear that a person should eat when their body clock says they are hungry.

Over time I began to face up to the reality, which was that the man I married was totally different to the man I had been engaged to. Did I make this fictional character up? It was so hard to experience the two versions of the man I just gave my heart to. Instead I started feeling waves of shame and disappointment of making the wrong choice, I held onto the good times I was creating with him and pushing away the bad times under the carpet, telling myself that all strong women go through it and this is what true love is, sheer devotion and commitment. I tried to convince myself that he would make little mistakes here and there but the agonising atmosphere between us would tell me otherwise. I would simply ignore it and continue learning what else strong powerful women should endure.

Remembering the year we had before we were married and throughout our engagement makes my heart melt and instantly my frown turns upside down. He was so loving and caring, and would send me flowers frequently. I smiled. Always pink roses, he knew my favourite. He made me feel like a woman. He took the time to understand me, my likes, dislikes and passion for my work and studies.

Jas was fully aware and understood how much I loved my family, especially my baby brother and sister. During the engagement period we would talk for hours on what we felt mattered in life. We did not always agree on everything, but there was respect for each other's views. It was refreshing to have discussions where there was a difference in opinion. I learnt how to convey my point of view and listen to his point of view. I always felt that there was a genuine feeling of love and respect between us. We would laugh for hours on end and I felt happy. He came across as an intelligent educated ambitious man, a perfect balance of masculinity, strength, softness and thoughtfulness. I felt like I had hit the jackpot and that all the pieces of my life were coming together.

What I did not foresee was what would happen within the two days of marriage. He either dramatically changed or he deliberately did not disclose this side of him. He was inattentive and unaffectionate. He became a different person overnight, and seeing him acting like this was breaking my heart slowly. I questioned myself and my whole understanding up until now. I had no one to talk to. All of my friends were back in London, and I couldn't just pop in and see them for a chat. If I did, they would definitely clock on to something not being right. I started to feel so terrible that I lost my desire to authentically reach out to them, I didn't know how to broach the subject and I didn't even know how to pretend I was happy. I would rather not. There would be too many questions for me to deal with and at that particular moment; I could not see the truth of my situation. His emotional abuse was isolating me, making me feel unworthy of any love. It got worse and worse as the newly wed days passed by.

The tradition is that once you get married, you should come home to your parents' home for at least a day, the meaning behind this was to slowly integrate the new bride into her new home, checking in with her own family for emotional support. My in-laws thought that this journey was not necessary. I see now that they were trying to isolate me. Maybe if I had made the trip I could have spoken to a friend and shared my feelings, maybe I could have plucked up the courage to question certain comments and behaviours by the family then.

At the time I decided to keep going and working at my relationships with all of his family, but now I wish I had called the police. It didn't even cross my mind. I know now the first time a man lifts his hands to his wife or partner, it should be the last time. I should have sought help or left soon after, but I didn't feel like I had anywhere to go, and I did not know anyone in this new city. There was no one in my life I had confided with, no one to give me the confidence to do something about my situation. I really felt so trapped, and I just didn't want to deal with the shame and humiliation, yet I couldn't stay where I was either. I was scared. Scared that this was the way my life would be from now on. I desperately wanted everything to go back to the way I imagined, I was open to do anything I could to make it so he would be happy with me and would not act this way again. I felt like this for three weeks so far. I even reassured myself and said "it's only been three weeks, three weeks is nothing".

All of this sadly brought back memories of my mother's experience with my father. My mother was a seventeen-year-old girl when she married and gave birth to me a year later. There was over a twenty-year age gap between my parents and this caused immense difficulties in their marriage.

As a young girl I witnessed horrible episodes of domestic violence towards my mother. I had a wonderful relationship with my mother and regularly expressed to her that she should leave my father, but I could never understand why she didn't. Now, however, I can understand the complex emotional factors and the intense desire to keep things together for the sake of the rest of the family. There is a huge element of denial. On one occasion I even called the police, when my father hit my mother really badly. I remember feeling so desperately upset for her.

She was a young girl from India, also away from her family, English was not her first language and she only had my father for support. In the early years he was her financial support as well, as she had three young children. She was totally pushed into a corner, with no voice and no exit strategy in those early days. I felt every emotion running through her body, and the sadness in her eyes was always etched into my heart, her diligence to continue normal life for my siblings and me was admirable, but there was also a strong element of sorrow amongst us.

Today, I really question my reasons for staying, knowing how I felt about domestic violence but even I found that being in that situation yourself is not easy to recognise what is happening. Only later or with external help certain behaviours can be questioned. In our situation, I was the main breadwinner because Jas was still looking for work. Looking back, I simply wish I had left at the first slap. But I did not leave, nor get professional help, and I did not value my safety or welfare at the time. I went through a lot of new confusing feelings, and I tried to convince myself that this was a one off incident. I led myself to believe that the man I knew would return once again. The kind, thoughtful man, who made me his number one priority. It did not feel real that he behaved this way so I blamed myself. The easiest way to describe myself was being split into two people. That this was a life of some other woman which I was watching and I was always waiting for my real life to start any moment now.

But at the same time, I could never understand what I had done wrong. The real question was why was I even questioning what I had done? Even though at that point I didn't get the help I desperately needed, my spirit was extremely strong, and I had the desire to keep enduring and working on this special marriage.

✳ PROFESSIONAL INSIGHT

The Bigger Picture Of Domestic Violence Abuse

Violence is often regarded simply as a criminal behaviour that is the result of a person's violent temperament, and that it is not connected to the relationship between the two people involved.[1]

Domestic Violence Abuse (DVA) is one of the most common, threatening and dangerous of crimes. It is the abuse that occurs in any type of intimate relationship.[2]

It is present within society, unspoken, but present nonetheless. In a report published by the National Office of Statistics, it is estimated that two million adults in England and Wales, aged between 16 and 59, experienced DVA in the year ending March 2018. Out of which 1.3 million were women and 695,000 were men.[3] Despite the police now being more aware of DVA cases and the increased willingness of victims coming forward, there is still a huge amount that goes unreported.

This book primarily focuses on DVA in women and we will use the terms, victim and perpetrator to describe the situations.

You may not be aware that it happens as it happens most commonly hidden, and behind closed doors.[4] DVA is widespread and enduring to those involved. Many of us may know a close friend or relative that has been a victim, or we may have even experienced it ourselves. Yet victims tend to think they are alone, excluded and different. You can actually witness it but not be aware of it. DVA occurs across almost all cultures and countries, races and castes. Even when stretching back long into history there has been millions of assaults, attacks, rapes, violations and killings of women in their own homes by men.[5]

DVA is a hugely disturbing and distressing picture if we care to even be aware of it. Many turn their backs from it, saying that nothing can be done. However, isn't it a basic human right to be living free from fear and living safe in our own environments? Yes it is, says The Human Rights Act 1998. In Article 3 it states that people have the right to not to be tortured or treated in an inhumane or degrading way.[6] Along with other important pieces of legislation that set out our rights to live free of domestic abuse such as the Human Rights Act, Crime and Disorder Act (1998), and the Public Sector Gender Equality Duty Commission, for Racial Equality Code of Practice, and the Domestic Violence Crime and Victims Act (2004).

DVA victims are more likely to be injured as a result of violence, require medical attention or hospital admission, and fear for their lives.[7] Men are more likely to perpetrate violence. DVA is also a major public health and clinical problem. Internationally, there are no constant demographic associations with domestic violence abuse, such as ethnicity, age and number of children, other than relative poverty. Although it is prevalent across the socioeconomic spectrum, DVA is more common in families and communities, which are relatively deprived. In the UK, US and Canada, younger women (ages between 16 and 34) experience the highest rates of DVA.[8]

To raise awareness, we need to first know the definition of DVA. According to www.gov.uk, the new definition of domestic violence and abuse now states:

"Any incident or pattern of incidents of controlling, coercive or threatening behaviour, violence or abuse between those aged 16 or over who are or have been

intimate partners or family members regardless of gender or sexuality. This can encompass but is not limited to the following types of abuse: physical, sexual, financial, emotional and psychological."

The physical act of violence comprises of physical attack and injury, it usually starts with a single slap or a hard hit followed by shock and disbelief from both parties and then a sincere apology from the perpetrator who says that it will never be repeated.[9] Unfortunately this is the beginning of the cycle of abuse and the acts of violence tend to happen again and again.

The cycle of abuse has four phases.[10] It begins with the "Tension Phase". This is when pressures and other conflicts initiate stress in the person and or the relationship. In a relationship the victim may become compliant to the perpetrator in an effort to reduce tension.

This may quickly lead to a snapping point and the second phase is the "Abusive event". This could take the form of emotional, physical or sexual abuse, and usually includes bullying, anger outbursts, fear tactics and other dangerous behaviours.

The third phase is the "Honeymoon Phase". This is where the perpetrator feels guilty for his/her actions and wants to be forgiven. He may even call it a one off event and make the victim feel loved again. He may overwhelm with gifts and promises of it never happening again.

The last stage is the "Calm Phase", the abuse stops or slows down and everything runs smoothly, he/she may still ask for forgiveness and shower you with gifts turning the relationship into a positive flowing synergy but over time the stress and strains crack. The calmness then returns back to the full circle. The cycle above can repeat itself multiple times even within one day.

Physical abuse can involve anything from threatening behaviour, to slaps and being pushed around, to getting black eyes, blue bruises and broken bones, to extremely serious incidents of multiple assaults. These can be life threatening, resulting in internal injuries, permanent disabilities and also sadly death. Strangulations are very common, and women been set alight, hit against walls, and kicked and punched along with being stabbed by knives. Some women bear the marks and scars of attack after attack. In many cases, the violence is less severe but it is almost always terrifying and deeply distressing. Women can feel violated to their core. They describe the humiliation and degradation of being slapped and kicked or being pushed by someone who claims to love them. Many women live in fear and distress, often alone except if they are with their partner and children isolated in the home. They almost always hope that the relationship will be better in the future or believe their partners remorse that it will not happen again. Some women experience violence, which results in hospitalisations, needing medical attention. For other women, the injuries may not even show. Violence also happens during pregnancy.[11]

Sexual abuse is very often the next type after physical abuse.[12] Women can be subjected to a range of sexual humiliations and assaults, and men frequently use threats of violence in order to make women submit to coercive sex. Only women can define the seriousness of a particular action themselves as it affects them personally. It can range from a whole spectrum of types of harassment, degradation and coerced sexual activity including the use of pornography.[12] Sexual abuse also includes withdrawing sex as a punishment. It is vital that women continue to speak up about these incidences and tell their stories. The trauma of these experiences can cause some women to block out their conscious memories for many years, especially if these experiences occurred in childhood. All too often they are blamed in some way for the sexual assault that has been experienced. There is no clear cut between physical and sexual violence, the two are often entwined.

Psychological and emotional abuse always accompanies physical abuse.[13] This includes intimidation, reoccurring criticism, withholding affection, verbal aggression, threats of violence, threats to end the relationship, jealous behaviour, accusations of infidelity and even destroying property. Children and friends can be turned against the victim. Being stopped from seeing friends or relatives is often what is a common complaint. If the victim is constantly being insulted and belittled in private or in front of others this is also psychological abuse. Excessive contact, for example stalking, using social media sites to intimidate someone (such as Facebook and Twitter) are becoming more and more common.[14] Research shows that psychological abuse can have severe consequences even after controlling for the effects of physical abuse.

Examples of financial abuse include totally controlling the family income, not allowing the victim to spend any money unless "permitted", making her account for every pound she spends, running up huge bills such as credit/store cards in his/her name and even purposely defaulting on payments.[15]

If any of these forms of abuse are left unaddressed then at first the victim may experience a serious Acute Stress Reaction.[16] This is when anxiety develops and there are behavioural disturbances within a month of the exposure to the trauma, and the symptoms begin during or shortly after the main traumatic event. Extreme cases include rape or other severe physical assault, near-death experiences in accidents, witnessing a murder, and combat. The symptom of dissociation, which reflects a perceived detachment of the mind from the emotional state or even the body, is a critical feature. Dissociation is characterised by a sense of the world as an unreal place and may be accompanied by poor memory of specific events, and in its severe form is known as dissociative amnesia. Other features of acute stress disorder include symptoms of emotional shock, generalised anxiety and hyper-arousal, avoidance of situations or stimuli that elicit memories of the trauma, and persistent, intrusive recollections of the event via flashbacks, dreams, or recurrent thoughts, and visual images. If the symptoms of the acute stress disorder persist for more than a month, and if these features are associated with functional impairment or significant distress to the sufferer, the diagnosis is changed to posttraumatic stress disorder (PTSD).17

Another understated common diagnosis in the South Asian community, are Adjustment Disorders, which are characterised by an emotional response to a stressful event. The stressor typically involves financial issues, a medical illness or a relationship problem. The symptoms may involve an anxious or depressive affect or may present with a disturbance of conduct behaviour (i.e. shop lifting). By definition, the symptoms must begin within three months of the stressor and a variety of adjustment disorders are identified in the fifth edition of the Diagnostic Statistical Manual of Mental Disorders (DSM-5). These include adjustment disorder with depressed mood, mixed anxiety and depressed mood, disturbance of conduct, mixed disturbance of emotions and conduct, acute stress disorder and bereavement.17

In any relationship trust is an important component. When things go wrong, trust is broken. Trust is like a mirror, that once cracked, will never be the same again. Similarly in relationships, if things go wrong what person can you trust? The perpetrator? The family? Your personal thoughts and judgments? After all, you chose to be in the relationships. There are no right or wrong answers as each person is at a different stage in their life.[18]

Once trust is shattered, there is no foundation of love and its extremely hard to form a healthy relationship without it.[19]

Gaining someone's trust does not happen overnight and any wounds and cracks need to be worked on and processed. There needs to be a time of healing and understanding. The victim might find it easier to process these thoughts with a professional. But at times letting go can be the hardest hurdle to jump safely.

There are many strong negative emotions associated with DVA. Dread, panic, distress and worry are some of them. Apprehension, hatefulness and nervousness are also present.

Fiennes (2016) actively talks about fears in relationships and how they can be painful and lower our self-esteem, resulting in us becoming weaker in order to be compliant.

Sometimes we enter relationships that we later regret. Expressing strong feelings for someone is easy, but the realities of life can sometimes make things difficult. In the beginning of relationships we tend to be on our best behaviour, but at what point do the cracks start to appear? The question is do you truly know the person you are in a relationship with or do you only partly know them?

This journey is a learning opportunity where over time you learn about people's character, working with your respective needs, and managing both of your emotions and expectations. Love grows on this journey. Regrets can be worked on, but at times these regrets tend to end in negative circumstances.

Change is an area where regrets can manifest. When a relationship develops into marriage, moving house, city, jobs and even name changes, could lead to regrets. It is not as easy as telling your boyfriend/girlfriend it's over, marriage is not a bond that can be simply broken. We can regret the decisions that we have made as our expectations have not been met.[20]

An example from another client is as follows;

"My husband used to take me to the cinema every Friday when we were dating, now we have been married for three years, if we watch a movie together on television, he becomes very angry. I regret marrying him and had I have known this would happen I would not have married him."

The above example highlights a simple want from a partner in a relationship. A victim can be in a dangerous position if the consequences are high and may regret falling in love with their partner initially.[21]

CHAPTER 2
MY BESOTTED HUSBAND

This was my husband; this was whom I was engaged to. So caring. So surreal. Bit by bit he took my breath away, again.

This time with love, excitement and passion. It was as if he had locked away the horrible one and this new one was more refined than he was when we were engaged. His behaviour towards me improved. I couldn't forget that he raised his hand on me, my heart, mind, soul and body had been impacted so deeply, the imprint of the attack never actually left me. The difference was that you couldn't see bruises now nor could I feel the raw pain of it. I did feel as if my heart had a huge hole in it, where my dignity once was.

I was experiencing yet another new feeling. I felt like I was talking and living with an impostor who became infatuated with me. It felt so fake it was actually quite scary. He took a detailed interest in everything I was doing. I started to realise that this man I was sleeping next to in bed every night, was a sociopath.

He took great interest in my work as a child protection social worker. I could only share with him some of the challenges I was facing, like working with families who were suffering from generational abuse. Due to confidentiality I was unable to share case details. He wanted to know how I coped with trying to make a difference to families suffering from issues such as domestic violence, drug and alcohol abuse and mental health problems. Jas showed deep concern and care for the work I did and placed me on a pedestal. He kept complimenting me, telling me how my work was so crucial and that it was such an admirable profession, and that I must be making such a difference in people's lives.

A few months passed by in this way and I carried on with life on some level going through the motions and taking each day at a time.

He would treat me with such honour, buying me luxury flower arrangements, and other expensive gifts, like extremely delicate beautiful clothing, rich boutique chocolates and the best custom made perfumes. He told me every day how much he loved me and that he was the luckiest person alive to have met me. He behaved like a love sick puppy. He could not wait until I came home and he would be all over me. On the surface I was kind of happy that I was being showered with beautiful luxurious things and getting so much attention and affection, but in my heart I just didn't want it to be from him. When he kissed me passionately a part of me felt like I was being raped. Something inside had shifted. Trust. This time, I felt I could not trust him emotionally.

My In-Laws' Story

They were jealous, it was so very clear. In the background, my mother-in-laws had observed Jas's smitten behaviour towards me and made sarcastic comments about why he showered so much affection onto me. In reality the tone and intensity of their jealousy was sad. I saw these two women; women who had never been made to feel that special or loved; women that spent their entire life sacrificing and pushing down their own needs, leading to huge amounts of suppressed jealousy and bitterness. Their comments at the time did not bother me, I felt sorry for them. They both needed an element of control because they could not control with their beauty, charm or personalities. Vadhi ma, demanded that Jas spend an hour with her every night before bed. How odd? I would quite often think.

Initially I saw nothing wrong with this, but the days he would spend time with me before bedtime, she would call on him abruptly, as soon as she realised he didn't go on his own accord, to make sure he came to see her. I felt so undermined.

Choti ma, his biological mother, was not bothered at all if he spent time with her before bed, but Vadhi ma needed his attention. I felt excluded when he would spend an hour with her, and why was it so important anyway? Why couldn't "WE" spend an hour with her every night before bed?

Another thing I found very odd was that Jas did not have such a close relationship with his biological mother Choti ma, but did with his non-biological mother Vadhi ma. He never even called his mother, "mum", he addressed her by her first name. But I noticed that Vadhi ma became upset if Jas called her "small mum". She insisted that she had raised the children, while Choti ma went out to work, and told me that she attended to every one of the children's needs growing up. So in a way, she was the rightful mother, and she felt like she had adopted Jas and his older sister Davleena.

However this was not an adoption, the birth mother was living under the same roof and was never called, "mum" respectfully. I found this very strange that Jas did not call his own birth mother "mum", which he did before we got married. So why do this before I was married and not after? I was baffled. These kinds of little things were becoming more and more apparent to me as time went on, and I really felt like there was more to the story, and there was a huge sense of foreboding hanging in the air every day in that house.

I was beginning to realise there were some quite disturbing family dynamics going on. I feel a little sick thinking about them now. Here I was being hard on myself about not stepping out of line, watching my actions and being careful of what to say or not to say and also having to make sense out of what this family was really like. As a new resident of that house, I realised that my father-in-law had his own room and my mother-in-laws had their own separate rooms. I soon discovered that my father-in-law continued to have a sexual relationship with his first wife! I came back early from work one afternoon and as I opened the front door I heard loud breathing and passionate screams coming from the first room upstairs. Clearly my in-laws didn't realise and carried on. I crept past their bedroom and into our room down the corridor. By the screams I could tell it was Vadhi ma getting sexual with the father-in-law! I was disgusted. I felt like I was living in an animal house, their lust was so carnal. I even heard her tell him not to tell his other wife. It felt so sordid. I did not want to be a part of this family anymore. The huge amounts of weird energy in the house, all these secrets and negative behaviours and ignorant attitudes; it was tyrannical. So clearly she had lied about all sexual relations stopping after her husband married his second wife to give me the impression of a respectable family. At that moment I was not sure how I felt. I soon started to see through the veil behind this "honourable" family. I saw how they were controlled by their impulsive wild nature. I did question why she lied about the sex stopping. I literally felt like this woman was a dishonourable liar. I thought to myself that it should have been clear to me that she would not live in the house married without having sex with her husband. I could never look at them the same way again, I couldn't even look at them in the eyes. I felt so sorry for Choti ma.

In our culture and faith a man is not allowed a sexual

relationship with more than one wife, unless his first wife has died.

However, medical treatment for infertility in India was very expensive and out of reach for many families in the 1950's, the most appropriate step was to marry a wife who could produce children. This meant the first wife was kept on in the family, because she could not go back to her original family and be a burden, but she could stay with her husband and raise the children they so desperately wanted. Even my own mother told me that this happens in Sikh and Hindu families in India to allow children to be born, as having children for a married couple was vital. The family reputation hung upon it.

Vadhi ma had previously explained her story to me. She was a young girl in a small village in India. She had been married for nearly fourteen years and her in-laws were fed up with her for not giving birth to a child. She described being called a "bharge", by the other women in the village, a derogatory term for not having a baby. Women in that position can feel a great deal of societal pressure to have a baby, and it is an immensely tough time for them and their womanhood.

Vadhi ma often used to confide in me and describe how low she felt and how she could not return home to her family. Her own parents had died when she was young, so family members raised her and they would not want her back. How saddening that this happens, even with family members! One day she heard the terrible news that her husband was going to marry someone else and she pleaded with him not to do it. Vadhi ma was devastated and lost. So she went to her family and begged that he marry a girl from within the family as this way she could remain with her husband. The girl that was chosen was Choti ma; she was attractive and very young so this arrangement appealed to my father-in-law, Aman.

Vadhi ma told me with flood of tears in her eyes, that if you did not have a child, even the village people saw you as a social evil and they would not let you near their newly married daughter-in-laws. So why was it so important to have a child in India in the 1950's? The main reason was that there was no proper elderly care system in India, so they had more children in order to take care of their parents in old age. Also in those days there was little government support in terms of a Social Security system like the UK and therefore your children were your financial support.

Arm Injury

The atmosphere of jealousy and bitterness between myself and the mother-in-laws continued and was intense. They were not comfortable with the affection and time that Jas was showing me. Every time I would pass them in the kitchen or lounge, I felt like I was about to get clawed by some very moody cats.

One evening, Choti ma pointed out to Jas and the rest of the family that he was spoiling me too much. Vadhi ma then added her two pence worth and said that I had never cooked a meal since I had arrived, and that a woman cannot call herself a woman if she cannot cook. How she became spiteful I do not know, maybe she heard me enter the house that afternoon! I found myself defending me to Jas in our bedroom later that evening. I spoke slowly and calmly explaining that I would love to be able to cook a meal as I do enjoy cooking, but I don't have any time left after helping out in the family shop after work and attending my evening classes for my Masters degree, which I was doing part time.

I should have known better. He allowed me to finish but as soon as I spoke my mind against what his mothers had said, his eyes widened and pupils sharpened again.

"They know best, you insolent little cow,"

he hissed at me.

Before I could turn around he quickly charged at me from behind and pushed my face into the bed so violently. He grabbed my arm squeezed and twisted it and I heard a huge cracking sound in my bones. He heard it too. At that moment, reality hit him and he backed away with the horror of the possibility of what he just did. I could see it on his face, he was scared.

"OH NO... I'm sorry... has your... arm broken?"

I lay on the bed for a while, face still pushed into the bed sheets, unable to move, unable to think, the pain of my arm felt as if I was hit by a car on the driver side. I was convinced he had broken it. Finally, a minute or so later, some of the shock left my body and I let out a huge flood of tears.

I sobbed uncontrollably, my whole body shaking. I sat against the side of the bed; legs pulled up to my chest, cradling my arm, the tears falling onto the deeply bruised skin.

I couldn't think. I couldn't move it and I was worried that it WAS broken. Jas said he needed to take me to the hospital immediately, and asked me what I was going to tell them.

"You can't tell them what happened, just tell them you fell, ok? Hold on, I'll grab your coat, let me take you,"

he said lovingly.

I nodded in agreement. I needed to get medical attention. We got into the car, and my feelings of shame were immense. Not only did I have a potentially broken arm, the pure emotions I gave him were destroyed. At that moment I hated him so much, I thought of ways I could hurt him. I couldn't. I was tired, alone and now had to lie about falling.

The hospital was a short drive and I was seen immediately. The staff asked me how it happened, and I told them the story Jas told me to tell them. Luckily my arm was not broken but clearly sprained and bruised. It was heavily sprained that I had no movement in it. The arm was placed in a sling and I was told it would feel better in a few weeks. Jas's face said it all. He was so happy that my arm was not broken and in the car ride home he told me that I had made him hurt me, as I was not listening to his mothers. He went on to say that I had made him angry and that it was my fault. I literally felt like I was sitting next to a man with multiple personalities. Once again I went into a dark dream like state where nothing seemed real and everything blurred into one; I couldn't think straight. I sat in the car silently nodding, my body and mind disconnected. I didn't have any more words to say to him.

I got back to the house, walking behind Jas, with my arm in a sling. Not one of my mother-in-laws or father-in-law asked if I was okay or if I needed anything. Instead my mother-in-laws gave my husband an approving glance and smiled, like their son just made them proud; that what happened was correct, in their eyes. On top of everything else, I felt a stab of annoyance. It felt like his mothers had "won" something over me, and the satisfaction that they got from this happening to me, was stomach churning. I would be lying if I said that at that time I wasn't thinking of hurting them severely too.

I went upstairs to rest, and as I settled comfortably on my bed, I could hear Jas and Vadhi ma talking. In a reassuring tone she said that I should have listened to them and that everything was my fault, and not to worry about my arm.

"Honestly darling, your wife is becoming out of control, she never listens, what do you expect from this London girl?"

They had no idea how torn I was inside, the depths of my indescribable emotional turmoil. That night he came and lay next to me. I could not bear being next to him and hear him breathe. I felt like a savage wolf was sleeping next to me, and it was just a matter of time before he pounced on me again.

Strangulation

I couldn't do it. I couldn't look at him; there was no way I would speak to him. What a monster! For days after I was disgusted with Jas, and I would deliberately keep out of his way as much as possible, for my safety. No one would help me anyway so I was careful of my every little move in that house. I did not even want to hear his voice. Just his presence left me on edge and every time we were in the same room I felt sick to my core with the fear that he would lash out on me. I missed my mother so much, I even thought of telling her but what would I say? Why would I cause her any stress. I wanted to hide under her arms and let her tell me everything would be ok. One evening when my arm had healed, Jas was talking to one of his mothers and told her that I was ignoring him and not talking to him.

"Why do you always have to cause so much trouble you silly little girl, I knew it from the time you were so rude to our aunty! You are more trouble than you are worth!"

She turned to Jas and demanded an answer.

"Why can't you keep your wife under control?"

This was enough to turn Jas's engine on, he looked at her and when I didn't respond to her spiteful tone, he charged angrily straight towards me. He really did lose all of himself in that moment and instead, the spirit of a wild beast entered his human body. He grabbed my throat with one hand and slammed me back onto the living room wall. His sour breath assaulted my face as he absolutely raged at me. He started pressing his rough hands into the sides of my neck, choking me. I pleaded with him to stop, and the look on her face was one of delight. She was feeding into his pride, taking back control that she felt was rightfully hers.

"She is being a cold hearted childish woman Jas."

She added some petrol to the tank;

"You are such a bad wife, with a terrible upbringing. I feel so sorry for you and your mother. What kind of women you are! You are unbelievably disrespectful to us in our home! You ungrateful girl! You don't cook; you don't clean. Who do you think you are? These "modern women" are useless, and you girl, you are the height of shame,"

she sneered.

This time, she too came up to me, and she looked at me up and down and said,

"You better start talking to Jas, or he will do worse."

I was fighting with everything in me to defend my mother's name, and to scream at her that their whole family was a joke and a con, and they were the most backwards disgusting people I had ever met. But I stood there, I panicked, Jas was not letting go. Choti ma triumphantly sat down on the sofa sipping her tea, flicking through a magazine whilst watching us, as Jas deepened his grip around my neck.

She actually genuinely enjoyed watching me fight for my breath. The background noise of countdown, almost mocking us, as time stood still again in this nightmare.

"Let me take away your voice for good!"

he yelled.

I tried to shake my head to get him off; I tried telling him not to do it. His anger was totally out of control. I whispered that I was sorry because I desperately needed him to stop. I felt the sweat from his face drip onto my arm, the smell from his dry mouth nearly causing me to heave and vomit. My mouth too was completely dry and I had gone cold all over my body. There was such a powerful atmosphere in the room, and I was counting down the seconds for it to be relieved. In that moment, the sound of the key in the door distracted him, and he fearfully pushed me away like I was a beggar. My head hit that same wall again, and I fell to the floor. He walked off muttering underneath his breath, and his mother came and leaned over me.

"Get up off the floor and clean yourself up, you look pathetic,"

she advised.

I was so angry I stared at her, and she started to walk off and laughed, this evil bitter laugh. For a few moments I just sat there, once again all the old feelings of shame and trauma overwhelming my body and mind. I looked around the living room, I touched the floor; and it didn't feel real. I got up and took a shower and changed into my pyjamas, and I looked in the mirror and saw the marks where his fingers had pressed into my neck, I kept looking until I didn't even recognise my face anymore, or the lifeless eyes staring back at me. My neck was so stiff and sore, where it had been pushed, and snapped back, and squeezed. I walked into the bedroom with a cup of tea. Jas had already got into bed and was asleep, snoring. What a vile man, how could he sleep so quickly and soundly after the acts he had committed just an hour previous? Am I dealing with an absolute remorseless psychopath here, completely disconnected from feeling and consideration. I got into bed and lay as far away as I could from him, feeling shivers in my arms every time he moved.

I whispered too low for him to hear me,

"When is this going to end? I have no idea who you are anymore, and I have no idea who I am either.".

I began to sob on my pillow, and I held onto it until I fell asleep with exhaustion and pain.

My Lifeline: A Little Girl

The next morning I went to work as usual in my busy child protection team. I had been working with a beautiful little girl over those few weeks that everything was happening to me at home.

She was a bright and funny little girl who spoke enthusiastically about her Wendy house at the back of the garden. The little girl's mother was in a relationship with a man who had been extremely abusive to her in the past. The man had broken her nose and fractured her ribs, and when I spoke to her she described some horrific acts of violence that she had suffered. The man was also the little girl's father and as part of the child protection plan he was no longer allowed near the home and if he did the authorities had to be informed.

On that particular day, I was asked to attend the home with a male colleague as the father of the little girl had called and was coming to the house. The father arrived and the police spoke to him outside of the house. The little girl saw her father from the window, and in that moment I witnessed one of the saddest moments of my life. Her skin washed out and became pale, she clutched onto the leg of another officer standing next to her and she crossed her legs as if she needed to run to the toilet. This beautiful girl completely froze and her tiny little eyes were so full of fear. She started to shake all over and screamed,

"no daddy, no daddy, go away."

This was the same girl who I had spent hours playing with, a little girl that was full of joy, but the second she saw her father her eyes filled with fear. The mother and daughter were moved to a woman's refuge for their own safety. I will never forget that little face. I went into the coffee room nearby and cried. I cried and cried so hard that she had lost her innocence. I fought back tears. Her mother had lost all of the control and dignity, and I prayed in that moment that they would overcome their trauma and be safe together away from this monster of a man.

I returned to the car with Hayden my male colleague and was frozen myself. He asked if I was okay and then I told him I was extremely saddened and shocked at how frightened the little girl was of her dad. I went into a rant, and he told me that the mother had been a victim of abuse over thirty times, only after a long time did she begin to involve the police. We both sat there in disbelief, wondering how it was possible that someone would endure that much suffering for that long.

I turned to Hayden and said,

"I could never have a child until my husband changes his behaviour."

And at this point he asked me if he was hurting me, I had to tell him, he just asked me. I told him the truth that Jas had only hurt my arm. He admitted that he wanted to ask me why I never spoke enthusiastically about Jas at work. He said he could tell from my body language that I was tired even before I got to work and something was not right. I told him that I felt ashamed of my situation, especially due to my professional role.

I told Hayden that before our marriage, Jas was such an amazing person and could not do enough for me. Hayden said anyone can paint a fairy tale but it is only when you live with someone do you know the real person. Hayden said that I shouldn't feel ashamed and he would help me if I needed his help. For the first time I breathed a sigh of relief. I immediately felt that this was the end of it. Someone had offered to help and right then that is all I needed. It gave me some inner strength. I felt warmth and connection with another human being; I should've felt this with Jas; something I hadn't felt for such a long time. It made me feel less alone; less crazy in my nightmare of a life.

That evening I went home to Jas and explained how we should not have any children for at least five years. He had spoken before we got married how he wanted to be a father to a little boy and girl and even suggested names. I convinced him that he needed to get a job first and we needed to save some money. Jas could see I was talking sense and agreed with the plans. Deep in my heart I wanted a baby sooner, but after what I had witnessed earlier in the day, how could I let any child of mine be exposed to acts of domestic violence, especially as I knew how it hurt me to see my mother suffer when I was a young girl. I will always be grateful to that little angel, because if I had not seen how afraid she was, I might have conceived during the periods when Jas was being nice to me. That little girl brought home to me that the welfare of the child is paramount, and it deepened my practice as a social worker.

Wifely Duties

I returned home that evening, with that little girl in my head. I was normally only home for an hour, before I had to go and assist Jas at the off licence shop until 11pm at night. They expected me to work there seven days a week from 7pm without payment. Some days I worked late and would then go straight to the shop, as social work was rarely a 9 to 5 job. On top of my normal work role, I was doing a child protection course. In that hour I was at home, there was an underlying expectation that I help make dinner, but often this was just enough time to get out of my work clothes, open mail and have a quick bite to eat.

Vadhi ma, however, expected me to make the chapattis, and I just had no time to do it. When I lived at home with my mother I used to help out a lot because I had a lot more free time. Vadhi ma and Choti ma would grumble constantly that I was not fulfilling my role as a wife.

They felt in the hour I was home I should cook a meal and then go and assist in the shop. They must have thought I was super woman! On Saturdays I would occasionally make a delicious stuffed potato paratha, a dish that Jas loved. He told his mother that I made it much better than Vadhi ma who made sure I never made it again. She then constantly tried to find fault in anything I cooked. Nothing I did was ever good enough for them.

Jas had been brought up not to lift a finger at home so never did his washing, ironing or took his plate out. Now I was his wife I was given the task of doing his washing and ironing. Oh how much I despised ironing his clothes. Jas would constantly fight with me for not being a good wife, but never understood I had no bloody time. I felt like I was just looking after a moody little child instead of a man. All my sexual attraction for him was lost, and I didn't feel like a wife at all; I felt like a prisoner.

Jas didn't care that I had no time, and would side with his mothers all the time. He would argue with me for spending time studying. Just after we got married he was so passionate about me completing the course. One day I had drafted an essay and completed the structure, and just needed to fill in the gaps; I had worked on the essay for days and days. In a rage, Jas came into our room, grabbed the essay and all my notes, and ripped them to shreds. I have never felt so trapped and disheartened. I was trying to better my life doing things I am so passionate about and for him to have the power to just rip that all away from me because of one of his moods was soul destroying.

"If you spent all this damn time on being a wife, we would not be in this mess,"

he bellowed.

I rushed down onto the floor and tried to grasp the pieces of torn paper, with the hope I could put them back together. Jas saw what I was doing and then picked up some of the torn paper and further torn it into small pieces. I sobbed uncontrollably, as the essay was due for the following week. I took the pieces of paper I could salvage and ran into the lounge. That night I stayed up the whole night re-writing my essay, with tears falling down my eyes. It was just so symbolic of everything him and his family were doing to me; trying to ruin my independence and my passion and my chances at developing an amazing life.

I was so upset that I was not allowed to study, as it was not going to be forever. I wondered what had changed as we had agreed before.

The next morning Jas woke and did not even utter an apology. This time I hid the essay under the sofa seat. Instead of greeting me kindly or with any remorse, he started talking rudely about my father, saying that just because my father had his head in books, it doesn't mean it would be that way in his house. He said I needed to enter the real world, where things aren't learnt from a book, and that I shouldn't follow my "dumb father's footsteps".

My father was an extremely intelligent man and loved reading various types of books and he was knowledgeable in so many subject areas of life. My father could hold interesting conversations on so many topics, not just in his work as a maths tutor. While I was growing up each room of our house was full of books, and my father's love of books had overtaken his life. He brought even more books after he became ill and had to have heart transplant. My father would say books were his entertainment and he could get lost in a book. Having all these books was a real bone of contention between my mother and father, as my mother loved a clutter free home. But inevitably his passion for them rubbed off on me, and I appreciated reading and learning so much. It was so frustrating to now be with a man that was content with me staying ignorant, and content with never improving his life either. It was everything I never wanted.

The same morning Jas told me very clearly I needed to think seriously that if I wanted to continue my studies the time had to be limited. I already had severely limited time and weekends were the only time I could fit it in before I went to the shop in the evening.

These demands placed so much pressure on me as I

scraped together the time to finish my assignments. Initially, Jas's family wanted me to come home for lunch every day, but I started to do my work in my lunch breaks. Hayden understood my position and allowed me to come to his flat at times to do some of my work and he helped me. I started lying to Jas about working late. Hayden even told me that I could make up excuses, telling Jas I had to go on weekends away for training courses. He said he would arrange it all, and all I had to do was tell Jas I was travelling with him.

By this point I had told my boss Jane that I was going through problems in my marriage, but I didn't tell her anything about the abuse. I told her about the pressure Jas was putting on me to not continue with my studies. Jane had known Jas since he was a teenager, as she used to frequently visit his shop.

So on the few occasions she visited the shop she told Jas that I had to go away on training trips or work trips. Jas had always liked Jane, so did not question it. But these two trips became an absolute godsend for me and allowed me time to complete my work. During this time I could see Hayden who had grown really fond of me and in all honestly he was the only person I could have a laugh with. We developed a very strong friendship and he became the only person I could share some of my feelings with. I did feel guilty for feeling so close to another person outside of my marriage, but at the same time he was the only person I had to talk to about the problems, and he was helping me with my essays, so I looked to him for support and care. I was trying to push down the obvious chemistry we had because I knew it was highly inappropriate, but I really didn't want him to leave as he was my lifeline through that period of time. The feelings of safety he provided me were vital to my wellbeing, and his humour got me through the darkest of experiences.

Soon after this, he told me he loved me, and that if I left

Jas he would be there for me and help me. I really just wanted to be loved. We spoke and I told him that there was no future for us, but he told me his door was always open for me. I am forever grateful to Hayden for his endless support and love in helping me do my work and for believing that one day I would pass my Masters degree. Hayden was also the person that supported me in the decision to not have children with Jas. He totally understood my position. He got me through some incredibly tough times, and the fact that I managed to cling on and complete my studies through such horrific experiences where at times I felt suicidal, is something that I am proud of today.

Left One Night

This was my marriage of six months, so far. My in-laws started asking questions. *"Why are you not pregnant?"*

Vadhi ma became worried that I could not conceive. She thought that people in the community would say that they had brought the same bad karma into their home again. What they didn't realise is that an intimate relationship with Jas was the last thing I wanted.

Choti ma voiced her concerns one day, when Jas's ex-girlfriend Terri turned up at the house. I also received a phone call from her. She told me that they were back together and that I should leave him. This made me desperately upset. How many more ways can he find to rip out my heart, trap me and disrespect me? I told Choti ma that not only had Jas been verbally and physically abusive; he was also unfaithful. The next thing she said to me horrified me.

"Well if Jas is seeing Terri that is fine, as long as he keeps it away from the home and the community doesn't find out, just accept it and put up with it as this is

normal male behaviour. It's not like you make so much effort with him anyway as you are too busy thinking about your studies."

A part of me was so angry, but another part of me was actually relieved, because I had no love left for him and wanted our situation to just be as smooth as possible while I carried on my career and helping people. The mixed feelings were hard to cope with, it was frustrating as I didn't know what to do, and I was trying to cling onto the marriage, and felt so trapped.

Vadhi ma was also clear that the situation needed to be kept away from the community, as Terri was white and they wanted the community to think Jas was happily married to an Indian girl. It was honestly laughable in a sick kind of way at this stage. I just shook my head at the level of deception and "keeping up appearances".

When is this all going to end? I used to ask myself. I didn't even feel like a human being, I was totally numb. Prior to marriage I was told I would be treated like a daughter and not a daughter-in-law. This level of treatment was degrading. Humiliating. I knew my mother-in-laws treated Davleena with total love and respect. Davleena would call the home at least six times a day if not more to talk with Vadhi ma. She lived separately from her in-laws and used to complain to her mothers that she had to visit them once a month. Both Vadhi ma and Choti ma would support her and tell her that she didn't need to go. Why was I then treated differently?

That evening I decided that enough was enough. I packed a few clothes and some essential items and drove to Hayden's house. I left a note for Jas "Goodbye, I'm leaving, I cannot take this anymore".

At Hayden's house I phoned my close friend in London,

Richard, and I explained to him what was going on. I felt really uncomfortable staying with Hayden, as he was behaving as if I wanted to be in a relationship with him, rather than focusing on the fact that I needed genuine help. I knew that I couldn't stay there. Davleena called me on my new phone. I told her about what Jas had been doing, and she reassured me that she would talk to her family and it would never happen again. I was so convinced.

The absolutely soul destroying thing I didn't know at the time was that Davleena too was not concerned at all about my welfare. She was worried about the impact that me leaving would have on her marriage. She spoke to the family about their "honour" and that they needed to get me back to the house before people found out what had been happening. She told me to tell my mother that we would all arrange a family meeting.

I really didn't want to hurt my mother, but I was desperate. I needed to tell her my version of events but first I quickly returned to the house.

I was so scared to walk through the front door; I took off my shoes and walked into the lounge. Everyone was so nice to me. Choti ma asked me if I wanted anything to eat or drink. She said that she was sorry for what she had said about Jas's ex-girlfriend. She also said that Jas explained to her that the calls were not from Terri, but someone playing games on the phone. The reason that he gave was that Terri was upset that their relationship was over, so was probably getting a friend to stir things up for us. Jas was conveniently at the off license shop this evening. It was a great family show and I believed it.

✳ PROFESSIONAL INSIGHT

Warning Signs To Look Out For In Domestic Violence Abuse

On occasions, despite all efforts to avoid getting into difficult and dangerous situations, Social Care and health workers can find themselves in positions where they are threatened with or actually subjected to, violent and aggressive behaviour. Whatever the form, violence and aggression can have a profound effect on workers and their ability to function professionally. It will impact on the composure of even the most experienced staff and can affect confidence, self-control and the ability to think and act clearly.[22]

To help manage these threatening situations, it is critical to understand where this behaviour comes from, what drives it and what the person is trying to achieve by the behaviour and the form it is likely to take.

Violent and aggressive behaviour is linked to a range of predisposing factors for example;

- Psychological disorders.
- Physical conditions that may cause pain or discomfort or restrict activity.
- Developmental disorders.
- Use of alcohol.
- Use of illicit drugs.
- Side effects of prescription drugs.
- Genetic predisposition to aggression.
- Upbringing and family influences and culture.[22]

Many emotions are associated with this type of behaviour

with fear, anger, frustration, loss, powerlessness, and grief being predominant.

Aggressive behaviour can also be used to achieve an aim or a goal. Some people will have learned that challenging behaviour works when trying to get their own way. The most common expression is anger and loss of control, resulting in violent physical or verbal outbursts. It is essential for social care and health professionals to be able to recognise body language signs that warn of impending aggression, and danger signs that show that is no longer safe to be in the presence of the individual displaying them.

Generally aggressors who are aroused to fight do not launch into an assault, for fear of injury. They begin by using attack gestures. By learning to identify these signals you give yourself a significant advantage in being able to manage the situation and keep yourself safe.[22]

Warning signs have been identified through observations of incidents of violence and include;

- Direct prologue eye contact with a clear aggressive intent.
- Deepening of facial colour, noticeable even in those with darker skin.
- The head being inclined backwards to maximise height.
- The person standing as tall as possible to maximise height.
- Kicking the ground with the ball of the foot.
- The person making large hand movements close to you.
- The persons breathing rate accelerating noticeably.[22]

Additionally the person may indicate that you are the

problem and as a consequence begin directing their aggression towards you.

Danger signs are much more serious than warning signs and must not be ignored. The person will begin to lose control both mentally and physically. They become unable to listen or process information, and will not respond to attempts at calming. Social care and health workers need to understand and recognise the signs, as they indicate a strong possibility of attack.

These include;

- Fists clenching and unclenching.
- The person's facial colour becoming pale as adrenaline causes blood to be withdrawn from the extremities and into the major muscles of the body.
- Lips tightening over teeth; this is difficult to describe but in fact is a natural gum shield to protect teeth from damage - loss of teeth could be life threatening in earlier times.
- Eyebrows dropping to protect the eyes.
- Hands rising above the waist, indicating a readiness to strike.
- Shoulders tensing.
- Stance changing from square to sideways; this has been identified from police videos of incidents. A side on stance is a natural reaction to protect the major organs of the body from harm.
- Person breaking their eye contact and focusing on the intended target area.
- If the target is out of reach, the final sign of attack will be a lowering of their entire body before moving forward.[22]

Recognising danger signs is essential. The time to make a

space between you and the person, or to make your exit, is when there is a combination of two or three of these signals.

To protect yourself and manage situations of aggression and violence it is important to understand what techniques are useful at what stage in the emotional arousal cycle.

How to manage aggressive situations: De-escalation techniques.

- Apologise if you are wrong as early as possible in the process.
- Listen - do not jump to conclusions quickly, let them finish their justifications and explanations and seek to understand their point of view. Talk calmly and respectfully with the person. Give information as fully and honestly as possible and give the person choices about what can be done to resolve the situation.
- Be silent when appropriate.
- Remove the audience around the situation.
- Give them space.
- Stay calm.
- Get them to sit down, distract them where possible, changing the subject to something else.
- Use humour where appropriate, but not towards them, as they could become more aroused.

Self-protection; keeping a safe distance (usually at least two arm's length) from the aggressor, will minimise the possibility of assault or harm. A clear non-verbal hand gesture such as a "STOP" hand signal allows the personal space to be maintained.

Working with vulnerable children is a complex area in itself. Social interaction is required between multiagency practices and families. As social workers, it is even more important to not be distracted at work from painful personal situations at home.[23]

The Care Standards Act (2000), introduced measures to build competence and strengthen social workers accountability to the public, and they now have professional registration with the Health and Care Professional Council (HCPC).[24] The challenge for practitioners after qualification is to develop an attitude of lifelong learning by continuing to work on their professional development through post degree qualifications, alongside reflecting on their work with vulnerable people.

Social work is not about just "rules and procedures" despite the pressures from some to make it so. Social workers are present with individuals during some of the most traumatic and difficult situations in their lives; they identify cases of abuse at the hands of carers (by adults and children); they deal with crises such as bereavement; and the loss of physical and/or mental health. In situations like these, social workers need to be able to witness and support the pain of others, while at the same time not over identifying or projecting their own pain onto them.

In health care, if you are not able to protect yourself and obtain the relevant support, there can be serious repercussions at work.[25] Service users are not best served by social workers that are burnt out, have personal stressors or are too tired to care. Often social workers are faced with some of society's most challenging issues, that not only require them to be knowledgeable about the law, but also requires them to have a varied professional practice encompassing a range of skills and methods of working, that enables them to work in highly charged emotional situations with others.

A social workers sense of personal wellbeing in their role, combined with the correct support, is critical for the quality of their service, and for their mental health. It is important that given the challenging nature of their work, they can make conscious and accountable professional judgements and decisions. They should still retain enough capacity to care for themselves, their families, friends and enjoy their free time.

In this context, we have a qualified social worker that is helping a family with domestic violence and acting on accordance with a child protection order. She has been exposed professionally to DVA yet cannot identify this and take the correct actions for herself in her own situation. Could this affect her professional judgment and conduct? Could she be so detached from her own pain that she is numbed to the pains of others, and much less effective in her role?

In this case, the little girl that she was working with made her fully aware of the potential consequences of her situation, enabling her to begin to take personal responsibility.

CHAPTER 3
LIES, LIES & MORE LIES

Mother And Brother Visit

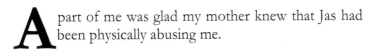

Apart of me was glad my mother knew that Jas had been physically abusing me.

Leaving for those few hours gave me the courage to tell her, and bless her; the minute she found out she came with my brother to visit me.

I sat across the table from them, noticing the deep look of sadness in her eyes, and the look of disbelief from my young brother. He was only 21 years old at that time, what impression did this give of marriage? He was shocked but was providing the support of a male figure alongside my mother. I looked at him and felt proud, I wanted him to realise that his older sister was strong. I told them that Jas had been hitting me and how painfully sad I was. My in-laws were present for part of the discussion but then left us alone.

They had all changed their tune, and that sweet fake mask was put on over the entire house. They were much more distant, I think they were just trying to maintain their pride. They tried to downplay the incidences, making them out to be less extreme. *"Every new couple gets into fights!"* they said.

My brother gave them a cold disapproving look, and asked

Jas why he was hitting me. Jas turned around and told him
that there was no reason and my brother exclaimed that this
was even more disgusting. Jas became such a coward when
confronted by another man. He apologised for his behaviour
and gave the excuse that he was "adjusting" to married life.
If I was looking at this situation without myself involved I
would feel happy that he was getting questioned and put in
his place, but the reality sunk in that this was my dire life, and
my poor family were trying to do the best they could for me.

My mother diplomatically asked him how he would feel if
his sister got abuse from her husband. He quickly exclaimed
that he would want to kill him. We all just turned to look at
each other, and a deep look of sadness and disappointment
was in mother's eyes. How could I have been so stupid to
marry such an ignorant man?

He said he was sorry and it would never happen again.
My brother advised that we should improve our
communication. When did he suddenly become wise? I
cannot describe how safe it felt to have them here. It gave
me a boost of inner strength that was slowly dropping off
again. The atmosphere was very awkward that evening. The
next morning my brother and mother gave me a huge hug on
the front doorstep, and left saying that they were there for me
and to call them if I needed them.

I was left with hope in my heart that things would change
and he would never hit me again. I felt like with the support
of my family our situation would get back to something close
to normal. Even my in-laws reassured my mother everything
would be fine; and the last thing they wanted was for us to
separate and the whole of the Asian community talking about
them.

Vadhi ma said no one in the community had ever
divorced, as they had held onto their Asian values for a long

time, hence why the families were so happy there. Vadhi ma added that they did not want to bring shame on the family through me leaving the family home. My mother said as nicely as possible that my welfare was at stake and in all reality she could not give a toss what people think. She went onto say that no one leaves their marital home unless they are pushed to. People get married with the hope that the marriage will be a success not a failure.

Choti ma wanted my mother to tell me off for leaving that night. But my mother refused, and asked her to look at it from my point of view. She told them I couldn't take it anymore, and that I didn't want to be hit again. She told them that she was entrusting them with my safety and that she never wanted to hear a repeat of this situation. I felt a tinge of pride that my mother stood up to those two witches.

The Backlash Of My Mother's Words

Well what can I say, what was to come next hurt more than the physical violence. Jas did keep his promise to my family of not hitting me; but he started to verbally abuse my parents.

When my parents separated and my mother left my father, she ended up living in various bed and breakfasts, and finally was given a council flat. Jas started to say to me that I had come from the gutter and I was pure dirt. That he had brought this dirt to live in his house; a house I could never have dreamed of before. I was council trash who had made it big by marrying him. Jas then started to say I was used up goods, and that no one wanted me.

He was referring to when I was seventeen and my parents took me to India. I was going out with a boy that my father did not approve of as he felt that he was no good for me. My father told the family that we were going to visit my maternal grandmother who was unwell. He never even told my mother the intention he had of me getting married to someone in India.

It was only when I arrived that my travel documents were kept away from me and I was forced to marry a man and was told that only then could I come back to England. I did not want to stay in India and therefore I was married and as soon as I arrived back to England, I ran away from my parents and moved to a hostel for girls who were also forced to marry against their will.

The hostel helped me to get legal advice and I managed to get the marriage annulled. This was a really complex time for me as in that year I was away from my family; I spent a lot of time at my boyfriend's parents' home. I had gone back to the same boyfriend my father did not want me to be with. However, I soon discovered the family were cold and unfriendly.

Not long after that, I ended the relationship and made contact with my mother at her workplace. It was only then I found out that my parents were separated and my mother had taken my siblings. I moved back in with them even though I was in the process of buying a flat. That year away from my family was a blessing in disguise, as my mother left my abusive father and I learnt to become an independent woman. I experienced providing for myself, and paying rent and bills. So I returned to my mother a very strong lady, who had also managed to get my marriage annulled. My mother supported the annulment, as she never understood my father's real intention of going to India. Also me leaving the family home and my forced marriage became a huge dispute between my parents, so my mother left as she did not want her youngest children to be impacted by my father's behaviour. My mother felt guilt about the forced marriage and felt totally helpless. We spoke about her helplessness and our relationship became much stronger as mother and daughter.

Prior to marriage I had shared everything with Jas about what happened and why I was forced to marry a stranger. His response prior to marriage was that I was a brave woman to have experienced and survived this ordeal. But now it had become a topic of emotional torture. He had absolutely no principles or standards, when it came to the lengths he would go to put me down.

Not a single day would go by without Jas calling me council trash and used goods that he had picked up from the gutter. He had changed tactic and rather than hitting me he was verbally abusing me on a daily basis. I questioned if I was council trash, and he was slowly eating away at my self-worth.

I let myself believe what he was telling me, and I stigmatised myself, but the reality was that our family was part of an abusive situation and my mother done what she had to do to protect us, and I left home and brought my own flat, and I worked for everything that I had. I had my own car, and my flat was producing an income when I moved to be with Jas.

I had completed a social work qualification and was in a well-paid job for my area. But I could not see any of these qualities in me. Jas had belittled me incessantly to the point that I had lost my self-worth and could not see myself anymore.

He would constantly tell me how my mother raised me very badly. He and his family were furious when my mother said she didn't care what other people would think. He used the point that she was a single mother, and it was so demoralising. He called her a useless human being who left her lovely home to raise children in bed and breakfasts and then a council flat. My heart also went out to all the women in similar predicaments as our family were in, and I was so disgusted by Jas's intolerant attitude. He was no man of integrity nor faith.

He didn't approve that my mother had friends from all kinds of backgrounds and that she had male friends. He attacked her character and wanted me more, more to distance myself from her, he told me he thought that she wanted our marriage to end and it was unhealthy to have her around. It was so awful to hear these things, as I knew that she was a gentle, kind soul, and she struggled so much when we were living with my father. She did an incredible job providing for us and worked very hard in a hospital as a ward clerk.

Prior to marriage Jas showed to me that he saw my mother as someone to be admired for leaving an abusive marriage and that she had done a great job in raising us. However this view all changed when my mother did not agree with his parents and her lack of interest in what people would say. This family were basically people who were utterly intolerant and abusive towards anyone who didn't agree with their way of thinking.

Jas started to monitor the calls my mother made to me. She would normally call on a Saturday morning for about 5 minutes to check all was well. Jas and Choti ma would hover around me to make sure I did not say anything unusual to her.

Truth Reveals

On one occasion, Davleena and her husband were visiting and my father-in-law started to argue with Choti ma. At the time Vadhi ma was in hospital. The argument escalated and he slapped her across the face and then kicked down a bedroom door leaving huge dents in it. He had been out drinking and was shouting a lot. Even his children's attempts to calm him down failed. Davleena let the cat out of the bag by asking Jas if their father was still hitting Choti ma. Jas responded that he was but it hadn't happened for a while.

That night Davleena told me her family story. Her father had been abusive towards both mothers but in particular Choti ma, for many years. Davleena said her father never worked for over 25 years and he had a job only for a short period when he arrived in the country. Davleena went on to describe to me that the burden of providing for the family fell on Choti ma and the children. The children had worked in the shop and prior to that a market stall from the age of eight. Davleena told me how tough life was coming home from school and having to go straight to the shop.

The family painted such an illusion of functionality and respectability, one where they all got on and loved each other so much. The bitter truth hit me that this was an extremely dysfunctional family. This deepened the respect I had for my mother; all the sacrifices she made to allow us to discover ourselves whilst not placing any expectations on us for the future.

My in-laws were the exact opposite. Jas was being heavily relied upon to keep the shop going and wasn't merely lending a hand. If he did not run it they would not have been able to survive financially, so he was never going to find another job. I had been lied to that he was applying for professional career opportunities. On top of this, he wasn't getting paid a penny.

I realised how dire the situation was, and that if I had known the truth I wouldn't have ever wanted to be there. I always wanted my husband to work and bring in an income.

I had seen the impact on my mother of being the sole breadwinner after my father had to have a heart transplant.

Honesty vs Dishonesty

Prior to our marriage, Jas knew everything about me; I was an open book. All my struggles, and all the ways I had turned my life around for the better. How I left home and went to night school. I felt in my heart that I had to be authentic about my past, my goals and aspirations, in what would be the most important committed relationship of my life.

It hurt me very deeply when I learnt that my father-in-law was an alcoholic and an abusive man. Jas was the family's main source of income. Jas worked all hours under the sun, and was rewarded with basic shelter and food, as if he was working in a 19th Century workhouse. We lived in a comfortable home but his life was controlled entirely by the family.

So he was a 26-year-old little puppet boy who did everything they told him to, because if he didn't, he would have nowhere to live. He had no voice to challenge them. He couldn't make money to move out and better his situation for us. He was like the golden hen producing golden eggs for Vadhi ma and Choti ma. He dealt with the accountant and all professional aspects of the business as Choti ma couldn't speak good enough English. And the worst thing about it is that he couldn't see any problem with the situation. He saw it as his role, and didn't feel that having a life with me was a priority at all. His mothers were completely selfish, and didn't want him to apply for jobs and move on at all; they were spinning a huge lie. Choti ma wanted to go on big shopping sprees to buy expensive things for herself and her daughter.

Jas was the same, and he would run up big credit card bills. Despite this, he told me that the shop was going through a bad patch and that he would need some capital to buy stock. This was the first time I loaned him £2,000 to buy alcohol for the off licence. In the back of mind I was so disappointed that they had lied about having a successful business, but at the time I felt like I could help them get back on their feet.

I was promised that they would pay me back, but afterwards Choti ma said that it was my duty to help out, and that Jas would always value his mother's welfare over mine. They were outraged that Davleena's husband wanted to spend a night with his mother each week, as they thought his priority should be Davleena. So they were acting like cruel hypocrites.

✳ PROFESSIONAL INSIGHT

Cultural Barriers To Accessing Help

Although domestic violence occurs across all ethnic groups, cultural differences impact on the access to services to provide effective intervention. Service providers therefore need to be aware that women of South Asian origin may have specific issues that need to be considered.

Evidence suggests that South Asian women and girls experience specific problems in relation to domestic and family violence in addition to the patriarchal racism we experience as members of the Black and Ethnic Minority communities in England.[26]

South Asian refers to women of Indian, Pakistani and Bangladeshi heritage including those who have come to England via East Africa. South Asian women in England are an extremely diverse group whose individual experiences are shaped by their age, gender, class/ caste, religion, cultural practices and traditions and rural-urban origins as well as their common experience of colonialism, racism and similar patriarchal systems.

In South Asian women it is important to recognise two factors; that the perpetrator may or may not be sexually abusive and may not necessarily be male. They are victims of abuse from other women of different ethnicities.[27]

South Asian people belong to collectivistic cultures where the individual is seen as interdependent and related to others and not autonomous and separated from others. What is needed is a framework that is reflective of the social, political and psycho cultural systems they inhabit. Asian women experiencing domestic violence are often doubly victimised, first by the abuse and then by their community. Amongst Asians, the family (extended over numerous households) is a fundamental and influential foundation, providing financial support and emotional security.

The accomplishments of an Asian family are judged in terms of the family as a whole, so privacy or independence is seen as undesirable. Gender stereotypes are highly conventional. Women are held responsible for maintaining family honour, a phenomenon known as "izzat", whilst avoiding "sharam" (shame). An obligation to maintain "izzat" can keep Asian women trapped in violent relationships.

Women who stay at home and obey their fathers, husbands and elders usually gain more respect than women who assert their independence, no matter how accomplished.[27]

Asian women in the UK have to cope with conflicting roles and trying to live in a dominant society whilst maintaining their cultural identity.

Despite differences due to community, class/caste, and the different trajectories of migration and religion, South Asian women share common cultural traditions in relation to family values.[27]

Their stories of surviving abuse, parental control, negotiating culture and religious rules are extremely similar. Contesting and challenging as well as accommodating ethnocentrism in families and communities, are also alike. The most distinctive feature of their experience, the element that underpins the variations in their individual experiences, is the overarching influence of Patriarchal beliefs and systems.

The power of the fathers and male elders within the wider

family is perceived to be a major factor in the abuse they experienced- ranging from coercion and control in family and other social settings to more severe forms of physical abuse. Ritual and tradition were also high on the list of factors that were significant in their abuse. In particular, the dowry system, arranged marriages and the concept of "izzat" were cited as prime examples of the exertion of patriarchal power and control.[27]

Arranged marriages have attracted a lot of media attention, usually being sensationalised as forced marriages. The custom of arranged marriages has to be understood in the context of South Asian cultural values, family structures and traditions. South Asian researchers have demonstrated that generally young people accept arranged marriages.[28]

It is often thought that the individual has no choice over their partner, but this is not the case. The majority of couples accept cultural practices and are expected to have a say in choosing their partners. Anwar (1998), proposed that class is an important factor in the acceptance of arranged marriages by young people. He reports greater acceptance of arranged marriages among young people from middle-class families than working- class young people. This is ascribed to greater communication and discussion between parents and young people and flexibility in parental attitudes.[29]

The dowry is an important element of the arranged marriage and remains the most common cause of harassment inflicted on daughter-in-laws by the women of the family. Giving a dowry is a traditional Indian practice that involves the giving of gifts by parents to the bride, usually in return for her giving up all rights to immovable property and the parental estate. Although there are great variations amongst different communal groups, it generally includes both personal gifts to the bride and gifts to the family. Despite inexhaustible campaigning by women groups and anti-dowry legislations in India, it still remains on the increase. Based on Hindu traditions, it is present with variations in all South Asian communities that ascribe similar terms to it- "Daaj" (Punjabi), "Dahej" (Hindi), "Jahez" (Urdu) and "Joutuk" (Bangla).[30] It is of particular significance to the Indian, Pakistani and Bangladeshi communities, despite not being accepted in the Sikh religion at all.

"Izzat" (Honour), is a powerful patriarchal concept used culturally to control women's freedom and sexuality. In different contexts it may mean reputation, respectability or honour. Although both men and women in the family and community should share responsibility for upholding family and community honour, it is women's actions and transgressions that invariably bring disrepute or "Badnaami" (infamy).[31] The family and kinship networks provide support and refuge from racism and oppression and this is used to control the social structures.

Although the great majority of South Asian families in Britain live in modern nuclear two generational households, the extended family and kinship networks are extremely significant. In the British context, the extended family has been seen to be problematic and it is only recently that the strengths of black families have been highlighted.[32]

Therefore in spite of the fact that the households may be nuclear, the family may extend across several households. There is potential for both support and abuse within this structure. The dominant figure, generally male, may also be female. In fact, women elders enjoy high status and respect and may also be instrumental in exerting coercive power over younger women to maintain patriarchal dominance. Another potential factor is the importance given to maintaining the family unit, which along with "Izzat" exerts a powerful influence on women in the family. When family honour is at stake, the invariable result will be in the collusion of the wider family in the abuse of young women. There is support and control, affection and abuse, in their experience of family and kinship.

In the recent years black feminists have challenged the assumption of the 'masculinity' of the abuser in relation to domestic violence.[34] Female members, on the basis of age and/or relationship with the abused, have equally been cited as perpetrators of both physical and emotional abuse against other women. However their power and scope of control is limited due to being female, as they are always less powerful than their male counterparts. A better understanding of these factors and the ways in which they impact individuals is needed in order to consider their implications in understanding the abuse of young women and also the ways in which they shape the help seeking process.

Religion and tradition are also used universally to control and subjugate women and exert a powerful influence through maintaining their social and cultural subordination.[35] Despite diversity in religious norms relating to women's roles and positions in their communities; customs and practices among Hindus, Muslims and Sikhs in South Asian communities tend to be more dominated by common cultural traditions rather than religious prescription. There is a huge prevalence of the dowry system amongst Bangladeshi, Indian and Pakistani Muslim communities both in Britain and in the Indian sub-continent, and it continues to oppress women and is a clear example of how culture prevails over religion.

Generally Hindu and Sikh women report more liberal attitudes from their parents and communities, although religion is given greater significance by Sikh women.

The dominant discourses about young South Asian women and their roles in the family and community focuses exclusively on cultural conflicts, identity crises and inter-generational problems indicating the limited understanding of their lives in Britain. Little recognition is given to ways in which the dominant majority contribute to the abuse and control of the young women through the cultural racism and maintenance of the myths and stereotypes.

The "cultural deficit" model promotes the image of young South Asian people as "caught between two cultures": the superior progressive Western culture and the inferior and backward minority culture.[36] Young people's internalisations of these images and representations alienate them from the support of their communities and does not seem to bring about acceptance and assimilation into wider society. Little recognition is given to the fact that they grow up in both cultures and actively act within and between them, rather than being forged by one or the other. The conflict hypothesis assumes that minority cultures are static and permanent, and are not fluid and dynamic like the dominant majority culture. These assumptions and stereotypes ultimately influence the thinking and behaviour of South Asian women who reach out for help.[37]

At the communal and family level, male hegemony is reinforced by both religious and cultural traditions as well as by the dominant society.[38] The particular ways in which these are articulated needs to be explored in greater depth in order to support young women in South Asian communities.

Our understanding of abuse in the lives of young South Asian women is extremely limited. Some studies that have been undertaken highlight the emotional and psychological costs of abuse and violence to individuals and the social costs to communities and societies. For example, there is some evidence that disproportionate numbers of young South Asian women suffer from eating disorders, the most significant contributory factor reported is perception of maternal control and dominance.[39] There is a significantly

higher rate of suicide among 16 to 25 year old South Asian
women that is three times the national average, and this needs
to be analysed in greater depth to draw out practice strategies
and policy development which is aimed specifically at meeting
the needs of young women of South Asian heritage.[40]

Barriers to disclosing domestic violence by Asian women
can be: [41]

- Nature of abuse - Threat of being excluded from or
  shamed by the community.
- Fear of consequences from being found if they do
  leave.
- Cultural norms - there is a fear of bringing shame to
  the family and going against traditions and cultural
  norms. There is a fear of going against the religious
  belief that marriage is sacred, that children need their
  father, and that individuals may become a hindrance
  to their siblings' marriages.
- Cultural pressures - Grooming makes it difficult for
  females to challenge male authority. Duty and
  tradition means being taught to respect authority
  figures. A woman is taught to be a perfect mother, a
  perfect wife and a perfect daughter-in-law, Girls are
  taught from an early age "Don't take your problems
  outside the home". It is a stigmatised practice to talk
  to strangers about domestic problems, and the view
  is that domestic violence is justified if a woman steps
  outside of her expected role. Women are taught that
  men are superior and therefore "your husband has
  the right to beat you". They believe that it is bad
  karma (against religious beliefs) to leave.
- Suffering is a part of spiritual life and sexual abuse
  can be justified if it will produce a son or "heir". A
  woman can lack support from her own family as well
  as her extended family. A woman married into a
  different culture and asked to convert to a different

faith can feel even more scared and stuck. If they do try to disclose, and not being believed is a huge barrier for these women.

- The knowledge that they will be not be supported adequately.

Self

To properly understand the concept of "self", we have to understand the difference between our "actual self" and our "ideal self".

Our actual self is built on what we know about ourselves; our "self-knowledge".42

We derive our self-knowledge from a number of factors, including social interactions, upbringing, influential experiences and aspirations. These are a few factors that determine your actual self. The ideal self is based on who and what you want to be perceived as.43

Imagine you wished to be an Olympic swimmer. This is your ideal-self. You can imagine yourself perched on the winner's rostrum with the gold medal hanging around your neck and your countries national anthem being played whilst they announce your name. You're feeling great and sensing what you would ideally like to be your "ideal-self".44 The journey in making the actual-self transform into the ideal-self begins.

Self-belief is the phenomenon that gives you the vision, passion and understanding that you can make this ideal-self. To every belief there is a negative and positive aspect, (Kohut 1971), which could either make you wish to achieve or not to achieve your ideal-self. As there are numerous exchanges between the ideal and actual self, negotiation is complex, and this is particularly difficult when there is a battle between wanting to get to the ideal-self and the actual-self not wanting to take necessary steps to achieve it. There can also be more complex factors stopping the transition.

So, taking these notions into account, self- belief is the manner in which you value your behaviour, appearance, skills and abilities. This self-value could allow you to make that jump and go for Olympic Gold or be destitute in an abuse filled marriage. Self-belief can be heavily skewed if there is pressure from external factors. In DVA, when the perpetrator damages a victim's self-belief, their self-worth is also devalued. How they value and recognise themselves is reflected as self-worth. Self-esteem is the method in which we view, think and reason ourselves.

Self-esteem can be affected by a number of different factors and these effects will differs for everyone. Factors such as being unemployed, losing your job, physical illness, mental health issues, a breakdown of marriage, divorce or separation and other series of difficulties experienced or negative life incidents[45] can put a negative spin on your self-esteem. This can be mirrored with perceptions that you hate yourself, no one likes you, you blame yourself for things that are not your fault, guilty to spend money on yourself and finally you do not deserve to be happy. These feelings if not addressed could leave you having a very low self-esteem and decreasing your self-worth and potentially being the root of depression creeping into the actual-self.

Argyle (2008) believes there are 4 major factors that influence self-esteem.[46]

1). **The Reaction Of Others**. If people admire us, flatter us, seek out our company, listen attentively and agree with us we tend to develop a positive self-image. If they avoid us, neglect us, or tell us things about ourselves that we don't want to hear, we begin to develop a negative self-image.

2). **Comparison With Others.** If the people we compare ourselves to (our reference group) appear to be more successful, happier, richer, or better looking than us we tend to develop a negative self-image, but if they are less successful than us our image will be more positive.

3). **Social Roles.** Some social roles carry prestige e.g. doctor, airline pilot, TV Presenter, premiership football player, and this promotes self-esteem. Other roles carry stigma, for example a prisoner, mental health hospital patient or an unemployed person on benefits.

4). **Identification.** Roles aren't just "out there." They also become part of our personality i.e. we identify with the positions we occupy, the roles we play and the groups we belong to.

CHAPTER 4
PHYSICAL ABUSE RESTARTS

It's not over yet...

I t was a wet dreary autumn day, when my mother pulled up in her car outside the house. She was here to celebrate our first anniversary.

She walked through the doors and just as she had placed her bags down near the porch, Jas eagerly told her how our marriage was getting so much better and that he had never been violent towards me again. It was as if he was expecting my mother to turn round and praise him! But she just gave him a blank half friendly stare and asked if she could get a cup of tea.

It was true that he hadn't hit me again. But how could I even begin to tell my mother about how verbally and emotionally abusive he was being? Her health was deteriorating and she had very little strength and I was so worried the fact that the stress of this still not making real improvement would send her over the edge. She was only visiting for a day so I decided to swallow my feelings.

She sat next to me on her visit and held my hand really firmly, ***"Where is my daughter?"*** Implying I was not my bubbly self. I told her that my asthma was playing up but she always knew that when my asthma was not good I would hardly talk. My mother accepted my explanation for being quiet, but as always her intuition knew better and I felt guilty.

The reason I was so quiet was deep down I was not happy with the home party and blessing at the Gurdwara that had been arranged by my in-laws. This was all a grand show. A show for the benefit of the Asian community to say what a lovely happy couple we are and for people to appreciate my in-laws for such a nice event. Inside I was deeply unhappy, and could hardly raise a smile for it all. It was not a milestone to be proud of; I felt like I was celebrating the first anniversary of being dead.

I certainly was no longer the person I was before I got married. One of my friends from London described that I had become a mouse, when before I was a courageous lion.

Choti ma had brought me a lovely saree to wear for the occasion. I could barely bring myself to look at it. I broke down into a flood of tears and held onto a photo of myself that I had sent Jas before I was married. I looked at my gleaming smile and healthy looking face and wondered where I had gone. I cried so hard wanting my old self to return that day.

Jas walked into the bedroom, *"Are you not ready yet?!"* He could see I was crying and he sat on the side of the bed and explained to me how I should be happy, and that I shouldn't spoil things with my tears.

I decided in that moment to tell him all the ways in which I was not happy, and how I felt cheated over certain aspects of our life.

"I hate your family home, I have always wanted to move out and build a life together like I was led to believe. Your mothers are controlling and self-centered, can't you see how they manipulate you to do what they want you to do? I don't want to be a part of this charade."

I think I said all this knowing my mother was visiting and Jas could not say anything to me. But, I should have noticed how his mood was changing, but it all happened so quickly. I was extremely wrong in thinking he would hold back. I briefly saw him tightening his fists before he had punched me hard in the stomach; so hard that I toppled over and lost my breath. He turned around, grabbing the iron that was heating up on the ironing board, and he held it to my face,

"One word of this to anyone and I promise you I will press this onto your pretty face, you will lose everything. One day I might just tell your mother what a useless piece of council estate trash she really is. Go wipe your damn face and pretend you are having the time of your life you stupid, stupid woman."

I was absolutely terrified of him saying something to my mother, and the guests were beginning to arrive.

Fortunately, no one had heard the incident in the main house as everyone was out in the far end of the garden helping my in-laws to decorate the summer house and outhouse, as this was where the party was being held. I was absolutely fuming, as I sat there finishing off my makeup, trying to push all the heated emotion down. I thought at the time how ironic it was that I was putting my makeup on like a mask, and also I was covering my personality and true feelings as well. I felt so helpless and alone.

The party was a blast and everyone had an amazing time, it was like watching an actual happy couple celebrating their first anniversary. None of the guests would have known what happened just a few hours before. They were saying to each other what a lovely family I was married into and that I was a lucky girl. The ladies spoke about how Jas and my mother-in-laws had bought me gifts. They told my mother that I never had to do anything around the house as it was all taken care of. No one ever really knew how I was made to rush to the shop the minute I got home from work or that I had to go there straight after. My mother was given the impression that my in-laws family were lovely and caring. But deep down my mother had already seen some of their true colours, and she wasn't convinced by it at all. She sidled up to me, giving me a loving and concerned look.

"How are you doing darling? It's going well isn't it?"

I looked over at her, mustering up the most sincere smile I could as I poured myself another lemonade,

"Yes mother, it's beautiful."

Isolation From My Mother And Friends

My mother had just come back from visiting her own mother in India who was not well. When she returned she fell very unwell, to the extent my younger sister called me to come to help, as mother had lost consciousness and was in hospital, and they did not know what was wrong with her.

"I am going to London tomorrow. Mother is very poorly in hospital, she really needs me."

Choti ma jumped in,

"But dear, you have a wedding to attend tomorrow. You need to think about your husband first and foremost. All the community will be there and your absence will raise suspicion. You can attend the wedding first and then go and see your mother".

I couldn't believe that they were so heartless. When Vadhi ma ended up in hospital, Davleena was there the next day.

I was distraught as my sister called me up again that day. I could hear her helpless crying and could almost feel the tears falling down her cheeks, the uncertainty of the situation causing her such fear. All I could do was reassure her that I would be there as soon as I could get away.

But the family didn't let me go and visit my mother until four days after the wedding. I had no way to release all of my pent up emotions; my sadness and frustration. I would go and break glasses and plates in the garden to try and let my anger out, but it didn't work.

The minute the family said I could go, I rushed to London and went to my mother's bedside. She had just opened her eyes that day and there was joy in my brother and sister's face.

"She must have known you were coming!"

beamed my sister. I smiled back, hugging her tightly and breathed a huge sigh of relief, feeling so grateful that mother's health was improving.

While I was not allowed to go and visit for those four days, I called my best friend to ask him to go and visit my mother. While I was there I opened up to him and told him a little bit about Jas's behaviour. I think looking back I only shared a little bit because I was probably ashamed of what was going on in my marriage.

After visiting mother, I got in my car and turned up at his house. He gave me a deep warm hug and a reassuring smile.

"I wish I could change this situation for you, and make all your pain go away."

✳ PROFESSIONAL INSIGHT

The GP Referral, Leading To Treatment

One day I spoke to my GP, who was a lovely lady. I told her how I had lost all my self-confidence, and that I had no friends and family in this new town. I was having blackouts, and actually had some thoughts of ending my life because I felt so trapped and could not see a way out of my situation. I also wanted help to understand why I was staying in such a situation and I felt that my husband needed to break away from the claws of his family, as they encouraged the violent behaviour. So I desperately needed some help. My GP also explained that my recent blood tests had shown a slight deficiency in my thyroid, which meant I had an under active thyroid. She explained that having an under active thyroid can also make you have low mood, so she started me on Thyroxine medication which I would have to be on for life. It was so nerve wracking explaining all these things to her, but I felt so proud when I walked out of the surgery, as I had achieved a major step towards accepting the situation and trying to get help for it.

I was sent off for the blackouts to be investigated but nothing conclusive came up from the investigations. My GP felt I was suffering from depression and referred me to a clinical psychologist. I wasn't shocked as was relieved that finally someone was involved. It made the situation more real to me, more manageable. I began to feel like there was going to be a way through it.

I had a few sessions with the psychotherapist and gave her a background of the abuse that was happening at home, and how desperately I wanted it to stop. I spoke of all the dreams and aspirations I had of married life and how they had been crushed within a second. I admitted how much I so deeply wanted children, but could not until my husband's behaviour changed for good.

We discussed about the times the marriage was functioning and when Jas was kind and loving towards me, but I told her I could not understand how he was such a Jekyll and Hyde character. She was fascinated about my father-in-law having two wives and how that situation played out in real life.

I recall talking about how I did not want to take any anti-depressant medication, but I was advised to think about it alongside talking therapy.

I spoke to Jas about how I was feeling so low and that I was seeing the psychologist. He thought it was a good idea as this may help me comes to terms with what Jas's true situation was like rather than the one he painted before the marriage.

I told Jas I was willing to work at our marriage and not leave, but he had to attend some sessions with me. I explained I had to be open about the abuse and I wanted him to get help.

Surprisingly, he agreed to attend with me. He was so unpredictable; sometimes rational, sometimes totally irrational. I could not really understand what triggered his behaviour, and at the time I thought if we could identify it, perhaps we could have a chance at overcoming our issues and strengthening our marriage. I knew the family were really making the situation a lot worse, and I really wanted us to get out of the family home, and often wondered what life would be like if we had our own space. Would he go back to the man I had first met? I was willing to try anything, and on a spiritual level I wanted to save our marriage. He had such an unhealthy attachment and relationship to his family members and I really felt like if the marriage was going to go anywhere, we would have to take back full control and create healthy dynamics.

By the time I saw the psychologist I had been married two years, and instead of seeing improvement in the family, all I could see was deterioration with elements of respite. But for the first time in those two years I had a possible light at the end of the tunnel.

I was so surprised to see what happened at the psychology sessions. Jas openly admitted to hitting me and that he did not want to do this and felt terribly sorry after each incident. Not for one moment did he deny any of his abusive actions. He wanted our marriage to work and the behaviour to stop. He admitted his personal circumstances were not ideal and stated that he never really had a father figure and he was under a lot of pressure; the one that always had to be the man of the house. He himself was struggling with having me as his wife and the demands that were made on him by his two mothers. He felt that he had to provide for his mothers as they had brought him up and I had only joined the family two years ago.

He admitted for the first time that he did not like working in the family business and before he met me he used to spend a lot of time after 10pm at his girlfriend's house as he did not like to come home and be around his parents. He disclosed that he was envious of me and how I had a job to go to on a daily basis. He felt so crippled by his personal circumstances that he did not even know how to fill out an application form.

He was torn between the feelings that he had for his mothers and his wife. If he showed attention to his wife his mothers' thought that this was inappropriate and as he lived under their roof, he had to abide by the rules. He had no personal finances to leave the family home and was frightened to leave his mothers with an abusive husband. He went on to disclose that some of this frustration had been let out on his wife. He felt he was Piggy in the Middle and sometimes did not know which way to turn. If he did not work in the shop his mothers' would not have an income however if he continued this way he would not be able to build an income for his married life and if he wanted children in the future. Jas said that he really wanted children in the future but could not see it being a possibility in his current situation and he admitted his current living circumstances were not ideal for a child, as he did not want them to be around an alcoholic grandfather.

I was highly surprised at the level of insight Jas had into his family circumstances. I always thought he was oblivious to everything and he just wanted to please his family as they were number one priority but this was the first time I heard it from his mouth.

These sessions felt like a new beginning and that myself and Jas could start again. A strategy was discussed at these sessions where by Jas would talk to his mothers and consider applying for jobs and working in the evenings at the shop. Jas thought that was a possible way forward. It was agreed that he would look at other ways of letting out his anger, i.e. taking deep breaths or punching a pillow. He agreed that he would stop hitting me as he loved me very much and wanted our marriage to work and he told the psychologist that I meant the world to him!

Once again there was a real glimmer of hope. Deep down I had some understanding that spiritually I should work at my marriage and divorce should be seen as the very last option. I remember praying to God that night and saying, "Thank you God, maybe things will now get better and please give me the strength and courage to manage this situation".

Anger

Whilst anxiety and depression are clinical conditions; anger (like fear and sadness) is an emotion. The existing approaches to anger frequently acknowledge that it is an emotion and then appear to forget the implications of this in a maze of cognitive approaches and techniques. By far the most dominant approach is cognitive behavioural therapy (CBT) of which Novaco is a leading component [47]

The CBT approach is almost always called anger management. This despite Novacos own acknowledgement of three layers;

- General clinical care for anger
- Anger management
- Anger therapy

General clinical practice when dealing with anger identifies it as a clinical need and addresses it through counselling, psychotherapeutic and psycho pharmacological provisions; including client education, support groups and eclectic treatments without a formal intervention structure.

There are six components in understanding anger. These are **anticipation, invalidation, hierarchy, hostility, permeability and sociality.**[48] It is not a diagnosis in itself but a behaviour that should be assessed within its context.

This is the real struggle in working with people referred for anger problems, what sense do they make of what is happening to them? This is one of the key places where conventional anger management programs over rely on being immediately accessible to the person. Getting to understand how the person perceives their behaviour is only part of the task. **It is just as important to identify what the people who are close to them think about what is going on.** These people, parents, partners, friends, work colleagues have often spent a lot of care and energy in trying to communicate with the person. It is not uncommon to find that partners have ended relationships as they were unable to tolerate the consequences of angry outbursts, or they were concerned about the effects these episodes would have on their children, if they have any.

There is also a vast majority of people who are seen with anger problems who experience low self-esteem. Their sense of invalidation (i.e. they feel they have been treated without respect) is invariably rooted in their low self-esteem and their response to that invalidation often reinforces it. One of the key issues for people with anger problems is the growing awareness of the damage that has been caused to their immediate family/friends by their angry outbursts. As they are beginning to understand their own anger, they often become overwhelmed by a sense of guilt and shame about their past life events. There is often a particular focus on the damage that they have caused to their children; damage they are creating, that is an echo of their traumatic childhoods.[49]

Group therapy or group sessions help with this as a group of people with their own experiences of anger and invalidation come together, share and are curious about each other's journeys, they then rebuild trust and rebuild their understanding and feelings of validation. Over time when the invalidation is successfully challenged, the anger does indeed begin to be processed.[49]

The above is primarily investigated within groups of men. Women on the other hand seek help for their emotions more holistically. Women are more likely to suppress their anger or express it through somatic (relating to physical body symptoms) symptoms than men.[50] Men's responses to angry situations are more verbally or physically aggressive in nature than women. Gender roles play a major part in this. Women often seek help for their anger themselves as they are concerned about the possible impact this could have on their families.[51] Men, however, tend to be coerced into seeking help either by their partners who are threatening to leave unless they do something about their anger or they are encouraged to seek help by social services, emergency or probations services.[52] This reluctance by men may be linked to the observation that men consider anger as acceptable, even when expressed physically. Displaced anger can lead into depression.[53]

Depression is a frequent reaction to domestic violence and about 60% of women suffering from Major Depression report histories of domestic violence.[54] Reviews show that women experiencing domestic violence are four times more likely to experience depression than women who were not abused, especially if the abuse was recent or ongoing, and the more severe or long-lasting the violence, the more severe and chronic the depression.[55]

Domestic violence can cause low mood or depression through:

- Psychological abuse, criticism and insults that damage self-esteem.
- Sadness as a natural reaction to what is happening.
- Being prevented from activity (work, college, socially or at home).

Depression And Physical Symptoms

Somatisation may be important to recognise because of the stigma associated with mental illness in Asian cultures. Physical (somatic) symptoms of depression in Asian adults include headaches, stomach aches and weakness. Many Asian women report feeling constantly tired, low and tense, or "aches and pains".[56]

In the field of Psychiatry, a major depressive episode lasts at least two weeks and typically a person with a diagnosis of a major depressive episode also experiences at least four symptoms from a list that includes: changes in appetite and weight, changes in sleep and activity, general aches and pains, lack of energy, feelings of guilt, problems thinking and making decisions and recurring thoughts of death and suicide.

Somatic symptoms such as dizziness, nausea, and blackouts, are common in such acute stress reactions. Headaches, upset stomach, including diarrhoea, constipation, nausea and tense muscles are apparent. Chest pain, insomnia, frequent colds and infections along with a loss of sexual desire and/or ability are often present.[57] General Practitioners assess these physical symptoms and order blood investigations to look further into what could cause the above. It is uncertain whether stressful life events precipitate thyroid disease as in this case. However stress can aggravate symptoms that are caused by a thyroid condition, and make them much worse and take longer to settle.[58]

More patients with depressive disorders commit suicide early in the illness rather than later however more depressed men than women commit suicide.[59]

Disclosure to a healthcare professional whether voluntary or involuntary brings to light the abuse that may be occurring. Professional advice and continuous treatment can then be given and in certain cases, appropriate authorities can begin safeguarding procedures.

Most clinicians and researchers believe that treatment with a medication alongside psychology/counselling sessions is the most effective treatment for depression.

Antidepressants such as SSRIs are first line treatment options for major depressive episodes.[60] Most people with moderate or severe depression benefit from antidepressants, but not everybody does. You may respond to one antidepressant but not to another, and you may need to try two or more treatments before you find one that works for you. The different types of antidepressant work about as well as each other. But side effects vary between different treatments and people. When you start taking antidepressants, you should see your GP or specialist nurse every week or two for at least four weeks to assess how well they're working. If they're working, you'll need to continue taking them at the same dose for at least four to six months after your symptoms have eased. If you have had episodes of depression in the past, you may need to continue to take antidepressants for up to five years or more. You should always talk to your GP, prescriber or pharmacist if you are thinking of stopping your antidepressant.[61] A dose of antidepressants should be slowly reduced: over one to two weeks if treatment has lasted less than eight weeks or over six to eight weeks if treatment has lasted six to eight months [62] This is because although antidepressants are not classed as addictive medicines, they can cause serious withdrawal symptoms if stopped suddenly. These symptoms may be entirely new or similar to some of the original symptoms of the illness.

Withdrawal symptoms depend on the type of antidepressant. The onset of withdrawal symptoms is usually within five days of stopping the medicine and will generally last for up to six weeks. Symptoms of anxiety, emotional outburst, crying spells, disturbed sleep, mood swings and increase in suicidal thoughts may appear if medication is stopped abruptly.

Cognitive behavioural therapy, psychodynamic techniques and other modalities are also used. Couples therapy is successful if the couple has defined a common goal right at the beginning of therapy. It can help them explore why the couple came into the relationship, and what brought them together, how they communicate with each other, what went wrong, they can recognise how strongly they wish to work on these issues and help establish potential solutions. If anyone is on the brink of a divorce, they could benefit by sitting together with a therapist to come to common understanding, someone who can make sense of the dissent and encourage them to listen to each other.[63] Sometimes therapy sessions can salvage marriages, but at times it is too late.

Domestic violence abuse does not just cause physical injury but psychological harm. Many women refer to the effects of domestic violence on their mental or emotional well-being. For example, 60% of women across England who separated from violent partners left because of "fears for their mental health" and 31% of women in a British Crime Survey described mental or emotional problems post DVA.[64]

After separation, women most often stress the long term impacts of domestic violence on their mental health, self-esteem, self-worth and security. More than 50% of women in contact with mental health services have experienced abuse at some point in their lives, and up to 20% are experiencing current abuse.[65]

A meta-analysis of forty one international studies seventy five showed:

- A large association between domestic violence and mental distress (depression, post-traumatic stress, self-harm and substance use).
- This association holds over different settings, people and times.

- Mental health symptoms occur after the domestic violence starts.
- The more severe or frequent the violence, the greater the risk of mental health problems.

One of the most devastating life events that can impact on women's mental health is experiences of violence and abuse.

The more types of abuse (physical, sexual, emotional, financial) the more devastating the effect on Asian women's self-esteem and higher the levels of depression and anxiety.[66]

In a study of 88 Asian women attending a voluntary organisation in England, the majority reported symptoms of psychological distress including feeling constantly tired, low and tense. Their most typical strategy for coping with worries were to "talk to someone" and "learn to cope with it", although two women said they would see a doctor. In contrast, the majority who reported experiencing "aches and pains for no reason" said that they would consult a doctor although the over fifties group said that they ignored aches and pains. Alternative coping responses included crying, trying to relax and medication. 32% attributed the aches and pains to stress and unhappiness but the majority said that they did not know the cause. When asked to whom they would talk about mental health symptoms, the most frequent response was a friend or family member; 11% would talk to a women's center and only 6% would talk to a GP or health visitor. 14% said they would keep it to themselves. Only one out of six women who were suffering from an eating disorder had received help from statutory health services. Only five of eighteen Asian women reporting marital difficulties knew where to seek help. Blame, guilt and shame are also reported by many Asian survivors.[67]

Asian women living with domestic violence experience fears and anxieties of several types:[68]

- Fear in response to the real danger, threats, harassment and violence.
- Fear triggered during flashbacks and intrusive memories.
- Symptoms of arousal or hyper-vigilance.
- Anxieties about the future including risks of further abuse, managing alone and coping with changed circumstances.
- Fear of the wider community. It is normal and healthy to feel fear during and after domestic violence, even though they may have had to ignore or hide the signs. If a woman has been afraid for a long time, it may be that her body's emergency response to danger never shuts down. Even after leaving the abuser, fear may remain or get triggered easily by ordinary situations. It can be a challenge to separate fear of danger, which should be respected as natural and appropriate, from past fear or unnecessary anxiety, which she can bring under control. It is not easy to decide at what point domestic violence is in the "past" and that a woman is safe. Professionals should be aware that ending a relationship often increases the risk of violence. Many women fear their abuser's threats indefinitely. Only she can decide if her reaction is valid, or something which she can safely change.
- Fear of the abuser(s).

Here are some of the words from different victims:

"They bully me, insult me; his father tells me I am a bloody Indian. They frighten me and beat me. They did bad things to my family. I am terrified of these people. It's affected my health. Every single day, I am scared."

"I have panic attacks four times a week and it's very

painful, because of him."

"I ran away from my husband because he was abusing me and I thought I was going to a more protective place. That was the most protective place in the world for me. Things went wrong to such an extent, it was life-threatening. I was given a small room with flammable things in it. I was scared to go out of my room, to open my door or answer the phone. The walls in my room were already broken. My brother used to kick the door every day. My mother, brother and sister would order a meal for themselves but not offer me anything to eat. Mother made me wash toilets with acid, with my bare hands to scrub them. They called me names. I brought disgrace to the family. They would say I brought a curse on the family, they would say I am a prostitute, and I was called a demon."

- Flashbacks, nightmares and intrusive memories.

"The anger and the horror inside me comes back, because of the dream. It makes all my senses rise up, like I'm on alert all the time... any danger..."

- Symptoms of arousal.

"Staying asleep is very hard as I am thinking and get scared thinking how to get away. People shouting scares me; it's unpredictable."

- Anxieties about the reaction of the community.

"They will talk about it. They won't give me a place to rent. After they know we don't have a family, they will say bad words to my son. The neighbours will call me names. They will say to my son, "Is your father coming

back? Sending you money? Shame on you."

I have no contact with anyone (from the temple). I am too scared because it's hard to find which people are his, because he gives lots of donations. I'm scared of these people. His friends, his group, they bully me and scare me."

Shame Is A Huge Factor For Our Community

Many of 100 Asian women who were severely depressed and at risk from domestic violence remained isolated for fear of bringing shame to the family. Another study explored differences in shame-focused attitudes in regards to mental health problems in Asian students. External shame (beliefs that others will look down on you if you have mental health problems) can be differentiated from internal shame (negative self-evaluation) and reflected shame (believing that one can bring shame to the family or community) Asian students have higher external shame and reflected shame, but not internal shame.[69]

There are numerous barriers to seeking help for mental distress associated with domestic violence. Asian women in the UK experience greater difficulties in getting help. Although consultation rates with GPs are higher overall for Asian patients, rates of consultations for mental disorders are lower for Asian women than white patients. Asian women are more likely to talk to a friend or relative than to their GPs. They are underrepresented in mainstream NHS mental health services but will use Asian voluntary agencies.[70]

Barriers To Accessing Health Care In Our Community

- Shame and stigma associated with mental illness in

Asian culture.

- Fear of being shamed for mental health problems and feeling trapped by traditional values (izzat) to protect the family reputation, together with concerns about confidentiality.
- Confidentiality has special importance in small and highly networked communities; visibility is high and privacy difficult to maintain. Just being seen in a GP surgery may have negative connotations.
- Belief that the primary care team only deal with physical health.
- Pressures from others to cover up mental health problems.
- Attributions made about the causes of mental illness.
- Practical difficulties seeking help.
- Asian families can feel excluded due to perceived cultural insensitivity of services and lack of understanding.

These cultural pressures place an onus on an Asian woman to manage alone or to deal with emotional problems within the family rather than seeking outside help and bringing the family into disrepute. However, when a problem is associated with shame and stigma (such as domestic violence or mental illness) there may be serious barriers to seeking help within the family or community.

CHAPTER 5
JOB

After our sessions with the clinical psychologist things were looking promising. It gave us a new lease of life. Jas had agreed to apply for jobs and go for interviews and so for the next few months, I helped him complete applications forms and gave him enormous amounts of encouragement to find something.

For the next few months our marriage was quite blissful. I was able to cope with the negative comments from my in-laws, as Jas was beside me, and I didn't feel like we were separated, I felt like we were facing life together once again. We started planning that once he got a job we would start saving to buy a house. This would allow us some privacy and give us freedom to live our lives.

We even went on a weekend away to the borders to spend some time alone and it was absolutely lovely.

Since Jas had been applying for jobs, he too had hope that he would be able to earn an income. He once again became the man I knew prior to marriage.

His mothers were unsupportive and gave him the cold shoulder when he came home from interviews. I would keep his morale going in the background and tell him not to worry as he had to think about living his life too.

The day finally came when Jas was offered a job in an insurance office as a junior. This was the break he needed.

We were both so happy when he was offered this job and went out to celebrate, but his mothers hardly congratulated him. It became really tough for him, as he worked a full day and then went to the shop in the evening, only popping home in between for his evening meal. He worked all day Saturday and Sunday evening. On a Saturday morning he did the cash and carry run. So the only time he had was a Saturday afternoon and a few hours on a Sunday when his mother would take over at about 7pm.

On top of this Jas was learning a new job and the signs of stress started to appear again. His mothers were also playing the guilt card that Jas was not spending many hours in the shop.

They also hated that on a Saturday afternoon Jas would spend time with me and we would go for lunch. They absolutely hated that we spent time together. There would always be such an awkward silence when we would return.

During this time Jas said he was taking a good few days off and we went and spent those days in Fort William. These were the happy memories I have of my marriage. On this trip we spoke about our future and how we were going to put our past behind us.

I vividly remember a moment when we were sitting on the beach on a massive smooth rock. I was staring into the distance, the serene view and sea breeze washing over me. Jas turned to look at me, with a beautifully vulnerable look in his eyes and told me that he was sorry for everything.

I looked him in the eyes and knew that he was telling the truth. He reached out for my hand and kissed it and I nestled into his shoulder. When we were away from his family it really seemed like we could make things work.

Jas's parents felt it was totally unnecessary to spend quality time and deep down they were not happy that we were getting on as a couple. I would often get comments from my mother-in-laws about how Jas needed to be there for them too and not just for me.

Vadhi ma even exaggerated her illness so Jas would spend time with her on a Saturday, and she would make sarcastic remarks about me never being able to take him away from them. But I had no intention of doing this.

Back Injury

Vadhi ma and Choti ma were so annoyed at the attention Jas was showing me, and in the evenings they would say silly things to him; that he was making trouble for himself by showing me attention.

They started to blame me that Jas was now working even harder, by going to work during the day and the shop in the evening, but I had been doing this for ages and no one thought there was anything wrong with it. But when Jas was doing it, it was a big issue. Vadhi ma would keep questioning him about why he wanted to make more money when he had everything already.

Choti ma would complain saying that her legs and knees were hurting working all those hours in the shop in the day. Both of them would keep going on and on like this every night.

Jas would reply that he was learning new skills and meeting new people and it was really enriching his life, but Choti ma told him that he would soon get bored of learning and he wouldn't be able to keep on top of everything. She told him that what he was earning was not enough to support the house and family. She even suggested Jas work part time at his new job, but he said there were no current part time posts.

All this pressure was building up for him and he had started to take it out on me again. Little hurtful digs started creeping their way in, and then he decided to take it further once again.

"This is all your fault!"

He stormed into the bedroom glaring at me. "Not again" I thought to myself, wondering what I had done wrong. That familiar sense of foreboding came to me quickly as I realised he was going to lash out.

"Because of YOU, my mother's knees are hurting, she can barely stand; she's working like a donkey!"

I got up and tried to start walking out of the room. Suddenly, he yanked my hair back so hard, I swung round, and fell face first onto the floor. He had ripped a huge chunk out of my hair and the pain was excruciating. He then stamped his foot into my lower back. Violent spasms travelled all the way up my spine, and I was unable to move. I lay there in tears, terrified that he would come and stomp on me again.

The force and pressure of his kick left me winded. He left me on the floor and climbed into bed. A few minutes later he fell asleep. I was so grateful because that meant he wouldn't hit me again that night.

I ended up sleeping on the floor all night because I was paralyzed, and it was freezing. My arms and legs were turning purple I was so cold, and it was seeping into my joints and my back, making it even more stiff.

As daylight broke, he started to stir in the bed.

"Oh my god, what are you doing down there? Have you been there all night?"

I slightly nodded and stayed silent, as he reached out and touched my arm.

"You are like an ice block, come and get into bed."

I told him I couldn't move, so he picked me up as gently as he could and placed me into bed, where I had to lay face down. He made me a hot water bottle and put it on my back, and I eventually drifted off to sleep. For the whole day I couldn't move.

This incident reminded me of the time I was attacked from behind and subjected to racist slurs at my work, by a lady who had her child taken away. Professionals had gone with my recommendation to remove the child and she was furious. She hit me hard and it left me with lingering back pain for months.

I worked in a team where I was the only person from a different background, and I used to get a lot of racist comments. Being a social worker wasn't the norm for Indian girls, so many of the people I worked with had not come across someone like me. The people were usually white, uneducated and unemployed, and in that area racist comments were the norm.

The Dark Side Of Aman

If these attacks weren't enough, my father-in-law started to become extremely sexually inappropriate with me. I could barely cope with the rest of the family, and then had to deal with his advances.

It started on Saturday mornings, when Jas had gone to the shop. Aman would come into my bedroom while I was asleep and tickle my stomach in an attempt to wake me up. When this happened more than three times I decided to tell Jas. I said that his father shouldn't come into my personal space like that.

Vadhi ma overheard and told us that he was only playing. But Choti ma believed that it was not right. Even with the whole family knowing this didn't stop him. He started to come into my room when he knew I was awake and tightly hug me, and if I was in the kitchen he would come behind me and kiss my neck. He only ever did it if nobody was around and I really hated it.

One Sunday, when everyone had left the house to go to the Gurdwara, I had a golden opportunity to study. I thought no one was at home, but Aman quietly slipped into my room and came up behind me. I saw his devilish eyes look back at me in the mirror, as he turned me round on my dressing table chair. He knelt down and started kissing my neck roughly. He then stood up and grabbed my hair, pressing the lower part of his body onto me. He was erect and breathing heavily. He then slipped his hand underneath my top and tried to pull it up.

"You smell so good darling."

At this point, I pushed him hard, picked up my car keys and drove to the library. I parked up the car and realised the gravity of what just happened to me. I was in pieces. I honestly don't really know what happened in the few hours to follow, as it was a blur, but I ended up at the shop with Jas. I had no idea who was going to keep me safe at this point, and who would believe me.

I walked in and Jas was serving a customer. He signaled at me to wait. So I went and sat down near the back door. I couldn't control my hands from shaking.

"Hello love, what's happened?"

I felt like a lost child. I went into what his father had done earlier in the day, and luckily he believed me instantly. He went out to the back of the shop and made me a sweet cup of tea.

"I am so sorry, this will never happen again, I can't believe him, what was he thinking?"

I told him how we had to move out as soon as possible, and Jas agreed to talk to his mothers because they need to know what he had done.

"We are moving as soon as we can, she cannot be left in the house alone with him."

"Oh come on, you don't actually believe her do you? She is doing this to get what she wants!"

Rape

So months passed after this incident and the atmosphere in the house was ominous, and like a pressure cooker waiting to explode. Everyone seemed to be trying to avoid what had happened, and I was no longer talking to Aman. He would give me the most awful stares, and the silences were becoming unbearable.

The mother-in-laws were still trying to convince Jas not to leave and that we should have a baby to give me something to do, and for me to stop making up stories.

"No one must ever find out about what has happened, about these silly stories, it would ruin your father."

I overheard Choti ma say to Jas one evening. His attitude began to change and he started to be less and less supportive. That night I told him that I couldn't take it anymore,

"I am on the edge constantly Jas, I have no idea what your father is going to do to me. I can't spend the rest of my life waiting for the next attack. I will file for a divorce if we don't make some drastic changes and quickly."

I saw his face change colour as he squared up to me. He slammed his fist extremely hard on the wall next to my face, and he then went on to kick me and punch me in the stomach whilst I was down.

"You are going nowhere, I tell you what to do, not the other way around. If you go anywhere or tell anyone what has happened I am going to make sure your family is badly hurt. Especially your little sister. So you better keep your mouth shut."

He punched me a couple more times and then he pushed me onto the bed.

Lifting my night dress he brutally pulled down my knickers, his hands strangling my neck and his hands pressed firmly on top of my mouth. The bottom half of me froze. I was trying to push him away, but he had his whole body weight on top of me. I couldn't make a sound and I was so panicked I was struggling to breathe. I remember turning my head, my face buried into the bed sheets, and smelling the faint musty smell, and I realised that I was having an asthma attack.

When he had finished with me, he pushed me aside like a used napkin, pulled his trousers up and went downstairs. I quickly reached out for my blue inhaler and took some gasps on it, and eventually my chest started to ease up. As I calmed down I realised that my husband had actually raped me.

I went and sat in the shower and tried to scrub myself clean. I ran my hands up and down the tiles but I couldn't feel anything, my entire body was numb. I was sobbing uncontrollably but I felt completely empty inside.

That week was my graduation week, and what was meant to be one of the happiest days of my life was really terrible. I had booked to have my hair and makeup done, and I had a beautiful dress made, but the entire day none of them congratulated or complimented me.

"Thank god all this studying is over! Now she can finally take on her proper role in the house and shop!"

Choti ma glanced at me dismissively. Jas was on the phone making a business call. I looked around me at all the other students and their families beaming at one another, their smiles glowing in the summer sun. But the rainclouds over our family were obvious. I was holding back tears so I could keep both my perfect mascara and dignity intact. I felt so alone.

And so, I got my Masters degree. I planted a huge smile on my face as I took pictures, hoping that father was proud of me.

That day I reminisced about the day I had graduated with my social work qualification. I was so happy with my family and friends around me. My mother was super proud of me.

There was such a contrast between the two times in my

life. I felt like two different people. My mother couldn't make it that day but she was the only one who called me to say well done. I kept it together and she didn't realise how desperately unhappy I was. The whole degree felt like a waste of time because my life was so sad.

Cry For Help

One evening I had an idea. Jas and I were at the shop one evening, and we got onto the subject of stealing. He said to one of the customers,

"If someone stole from me I would disown them, family member or not."

On the radio that week I had heard a couple of times that the local police were really cracking down on thieves as there was an influx of crimes of this nature in the community.

In that moment I thought that if I got caught stealing and people found out, Jas would probably disown me and it would give me a reason to leave. Then he wouldn't hurt my family in London as it was him making the choice. It was a desperate option but it might work!

The next morning I went into a high street store. I very blatantly shoved two items of clothing into my bag. I walked out but no one stopped me. I started walking away disappointed, but then I turned round as a policeman tapped my shoulder and asked to look in my bag.

"You have a lot of money in your purse, why did you not pay for these items?"

Him and his colleague looked at me oddly.

I was taken back to the police station and was told that I did not fit the usual shop lifter profile. They kept on questioning me until I started to break down. Eventually I told them how afraid I was of my father-in-law and how he made sexual advances at me. How my husband and his mothers were unkind to me. If I got caught stealing my husband may disown me. I remember one of the officers saying that it was a cry for help.

I was placed in a cell for seven hours, as I think they did not know what to do with me. I hated being in such a small space and I cried uncontrollably. But at the same time I felt I was safe. It was such a desperate situation that I preferred being in a jail cell than at home.

Eventually a policewoman came round with food, but I didn't want to eat, and I told her that I didn't want to go back to the house. She looked at me sympathetically,

"Love, we know you haven't done anything wrong, but you can't stay here all night, we need to call someone to come and get you."

Jas turned up an hour later and came to collect me from the reception. I couldn't really understand what the look was on his face. It was like a mixture of surprise, sadness, and anger.

"Just come home now love, and I promise that within two weeks we will move into a rented place and we will be away from all this."

I really feel like I had lost my mind at that point, I was very confused. Sitting in the cell I started to come to terms with how irrational my actions were. It felt so annoyed with myself and ashamed. I felt enough shame in the situation, but I was desperately trying to find a way out.

I was later told when I went for some individual counseling and by the GP, that when someone is coming off anti-depressants they can feel a flood of emotions, that had been kept at bay, and when the cry for help incident happened it may have impacted my thought pattern. Eight months before I had been placed on anti-depressants and while I was on them I felt no emotions. No matter what happened my mood just stayed flat and I no longer felt high or low moods, no matter what was happening around me, which in essence helped me manage my situation. But at the time of the shop lifting incident I was weaning myself off the antidepressants as directed by my GP. While the weaning process was happening all my emotions were coming back. They came back so fast and furious that I found it unbearable to manage, I was now able to feel sadness, pain, fear, terror and so many more emotions that I could not feel while I was on the antidepressant medication.

All the professionals around me including the solicitor put forward the argument that this type of behaviour was a cry for help. They argued that I never had any previous criminal history and this incident should not impact my job. But it did help in regards to Jas. He woke up to how serious this situation was and realised what lengths I was prepared to go to.

Within weeks we had found a flat for us to rent. It was disgusting inside, but I didnt care as I was just glad to be away from the family.

First Police Contact

So Jas and I started a new chapter. We moved all our belongings to the new flat. I really felt like we could have a chance now away from this horrific family.

On the last day of moving over all our things, Choti ma started to cry uncontrollably. She came up to Jas and held onto his jumper. She even fell to the floor. I nearly burst out laughing at how dramatic it all was. Choti ma and Vadhi ma both started applying a lot of pressure.

Upstairs I was sitting on the bed, waiting for him to load the car with the last of the boxes. He came up and sat on the edge of the bed, *"Are we making the right decision?"* I defiantly told him in no uncertain terms that I was leaving that day.

For the first time, he hit my face. He repeatedly slapped me and made a blow on the side of my head. It was so vicious. He punched me in the stomach. He really went to town on me.

He screamed over and over again how I made his life so difficult and stressed, why couldn't I just do as I was told?

"I am not leaving, they are right. We are making the wrong decision."

Choti ma and Vadhi ma were hovering around like vultures. They had smelt blood and they were grinning. They knew their mind games and manipulations were working. Jas was so predictable and walked into their traps time and time again.

I grabbed my car keys and ran towards the door. Jas ran after me to the front door and started to push my hand away from the front door latch. I managed to get his hand off the latch and opened the door and ran towards the car. I opened the door quickly and locked myself in.

My heart was racing so so fast. He came storming out and he banged both fists down on the windscreen with full force.

I was so surprised that the glass didn't smash.

I tried to reverse quickly and as I was moving he grabbed hold of the wing mirror and pulled it straight off. As it fell into his hand he took hold of it and chucked it at the windscreen. It cracked it on my side, but I kept going. I had no idea what I was doing; everything was a blur. I was running off of pure adrenaline.

I pulled up at the lights at the end of the road, and there in front of me; a twist of fate; Hayden was at the lights with his girlfriend. They could see I was hurt and got me to pull over, and I think they were shocked at how badly shaken up I was. Hayden saw I had bruising on my face and I was clearly in distress. They took me back to their flat.

Hayden took photos of my injuries, mainly my face and then told me he had called the police. I was utterly zoned out. That night I stayed with them and it was such a blurry mess, I do not remember anything about it. They kept on talking to me to try and bring me back to reality and make sure that I was okay, but I wasn't taking anything in.

The police had visited Jas and warned him about his behaviour. I felt uncomfortable staying another night and went back to the flat. I was finally coming down off the adrenaline surges, but still felt extremely numb and spaced out. I just didn't feel like this was my reality. I was floating above my body as if I was looking from a bird's eye view.

I was sitting on the sofa. I heard the key turn in the door. I could just sense that the way he came into the flat that he was going to beg me for another chance.

"Vadhi ma and Choti ma are in the same position as you love, they don't want to be left in the house with Aman neither! I feel responsible for this situation. It is

not so easy, can't you see? Please give me another chance, I am so stressed and I have no space or time to be able to relieve it. I just want things to work out. I don't know what to do."

Jas told me that he was scared that the police visited him, because he felt like we were making a lot of improvements in the last few weeks and he didn't want to lose that. I had zero energy to fight that night. I had heard everything before so many times. He had turned my heart and soul into a stone. I didn't have anything to say anymore. But I did have hope that because the police were involved he would think twice about how he was treating me and that it may make a difference now we were away from his family. But it was all up in the air, unpredictable, as it always was.

✳ PROFESSIONAL INSIGHT

Analysis, Jealousy And Other Feelings

Jealousy in relationships can be a common occurrence; where a person can respond to a real or imagined threat with a negative emotional response.

The outcome of the negatively charged emotional response could lead to a number of different situations.[71] Individuals may be controlling and abusive. You may have a partner that does not like you talking to the opposite sex unnecessarily, which could lead to rifts in the relationship. Jealously stems from the emotions of fear, losing someone or something going out of control. Jealousy is an outward manifestation, which leads to heightened insecurity, which is an inward emotion.

Insecurity when broken down literally means the self-doubt you have about yourself.[72] It may be feeling fat, ugly and short which adds to a lack of confidence, leading to instability and therefore insecurity. This insecurity can then be projected on to the relationship, and this can damage the relationship if not understood or supported.

Physical abuse has been discussed at the end of chapter one.

Racial Abuse - Victimised At Work

Race discrimination is when you are treated unfairly because of your racial origin, "Race" includes colour, nationality, citizenship and ethnic or national origins. Race discrimination can be direct or indirect. It may also take the form of harassment or victimisation.[73]

It is direct race discrimination to treat someone less favourably than you would another person in the same circumstances, on the grounds of race. Racist abuse and harassment are forms of direct discrimination.

The Cry For Help

Kleptomania is a recurrent failure to resist impulses to steal objects not needed for personal use or for monetary value.[74] The symptoms of kleptomania tend to appear in times of significant stress for example when a person is experiencing separations or going through grief processes.

If emotional or mental health issues could be the reason for stealing, a person might benefit from seeing a therapist or mental health professional. Kleptomania is extremely difficult to treat alone, so getting medical help is a necessity for most who experience it. Treatment typically involves a combination of psychotherapy and medications, which can address triggers and causes.

Cognitive behavioural therapy is most commonly used to treat kleptomania.

In this case if the stealing behaviour continued then this could signal kleptomania; however, the aim for stealing was to be caught by police services as a cry for help. This was to escape from the relationship and in turn would bring shame onto the family, which would act for her as an escape route.

Police Intervention

It is well known that a woman is more likely to be attacked by someone she knows rather than a stranger.[75]

Police practice in domestic disputes look to quickly defuse situations and then they withdraw. This leads women to be open to more attacks in the future.

As far as the perpetrator is concerned, the police will not arrest him on the spot, unless he is in breach of an injunction with a power of arrest attached. Even then they are unlikely to make an arrest. At best they may subsequently charge him with an offence, but in most cases the charges will be withdrawn, usually on the grounds that the victim does not wish to proceed.

It is important to approach the issue of domestic violence with sensitivity to the range of situations involved, including both those where the woman wants to get the man out of her life forever and those where she wishes to maintain some kind of relationship with him.[76]

We are entitled to express our needs and the police must endeavour to protect us from further injury by enforcing the law when this is the appropriate action to take.

There are many agencies that can provide help such as Women's Aid, who can signpost vulnerable individuals to different agencies that can provide all the services that they may need.

In 2018 there have been many new exciting developments from the government that is transforming our approach to domestic abuse.

These include:

- Potential for the Domestic Violence Disclosure Scheme, known as "Clare's Law"[77], to be enshrined in legislation. This allows police to disclose information about previous violent offending by a new or existing partner, and builds better protection for victims. It has already been rolled out operationally across the country.

- Proposals to give domestic abuse victims the same status in court as those who have suffered modern slavery or sex offences, so that they would be automatically eligible for the range of special measures available in criminal proceedings, such as giving evidence behind a screen or via video link.
- Creating a statutory aggravating factor in sentencing, similar to those already in-law for hate crimes, for domestic abuse to toughen sentences when it involves or affects a child Creation of a Domestic Abuse Commissioner to hold the government to account.
- Recognising economic abuse as a type of domestic abuse. This would cover controlling circumstances in which victims have finances withheld, are denied access to employment or transport, or are forced to take out loans and enter into other financial contracts.

The Domestic Violence Disclosure Scheme (DVDS) is a scheme, known as "Clare's Law"[77] after the landmark case that led to it. Clare Wood was brutally murdered five years ago by her former partner George Appleton, who had a record of violence against women.

Clare's Law allows the police and partner agencies to carry out an array of checks once an application is made. Discourses may be made if the resulting information, i.e. records of abusive offence or a trace and danger of domestic violence or abuse, which could affect the concerned party.

It also gives any member of the public the right to ask the police if their partner may pose a risk to them. Under Clare's Law, a member of the public can also make enquiries into the partner of a close friend or family member.

In 2019, an official domestic abuse bill is in place to help tackle the crime, the new legislation will:

- Introduce the first ever statutory government definition of domestic abuse to specifically include economic abuse and controlling and manipulative non-physical abuse. This will enable everyone, including victims themselves, to understand what constitutes abuse and will encourage more victims to come forward.
- Establish a Domestic Abuse Commissioner to drive the response to domestic abuse issues.
- Introduce new Domestic Abuse Protection Notices and Domestic Abuse Protection Orders to further protect victims and place restrictions on the actions of offenders.
- Prohibit the cross-examination of victims by their abusers in the family courts.
- Provide automatic eligibility for special measures to support more victims to give evidence in the criminal courts.[78]

CHAPTER 6
BACK PROBLEMS

My back was getting steadily worse and more painful. Who knows why it was so bad. Was it because I had been hit by a client or was it exasperated by Jas stamping on my back when I was helplessly laying on the floor? I never told anyone about what Jas had done to me that night, when he attacked me but I hated what was to come after that day. Each day I was in pain. Some days so much so that I could not walk for periods of the day, as my leg would go into spasm. I would see my GP, who gave me pain medication, but even pain medication stopped working. I would wear a Transcutaneous Electric Nerve Stimulation (TENS) machine unit to work, so I could make it through the day. My work was my only refuge and I loved what I did. I was just struggling to cope each morning getting out of bed and getting myself dressed. What was usually a fifteen minute task, started to take nearly 2 hours in the morning.

I was in so much pain some days that I really just wanted my life to end. I would find it difficult to lift, do household chores, sit, stand and walk for longer periods. I was in discomfort all the time, as if I sat more than twenty minutes, the pain would get worse, and I couldn't stand for more than twenty minutes at a time. I remember at times I would be so exhausted with the pain that I would spend a lot of my weekends in bed.

I had to rely on Jas doing some of the housework in the flat because at times the spasms were so excruciating. His resentment was obvious and he made me suffer for it.

He made fun of me a lot and sometimes he would kick my leg and push me over, and watch me fall down and struggle trying to get back up. He would sit on the sofa mocking me, calling me a cripple, and he would completely humiliate me with his comments. He would sneer at me saying that I was unable to have children, as I was a stupid disabled person.

One night when I was sitting on the sofa, trying to unwind and have a bit of peace and respite from my leg, he started launching his usual attack,

"You are lucky that I stay with you, look at you, you are pathetic and useless. You disgust me. You can't even look after yourself let alone a child; you cant do housework. Of what use are you woman?"

He laughed at me and looked down at his phone screen and totally blanked me out. I was really glad that we weren't having children. What kind of life would the child have?

Jas did not realise that I was trying to keep my energy to be able to continue going to work, as I was the main breadwinner. If I tried to do house work on top of my work it was just totally impossible to do the both with my condition. So I concentrated my energy in keeping my job.

I did not view myself as disabled but I did recognise there were so many things I could not do especially when my leg was really bad and my lower back. I had good days and bad days, but on the bad days I really had to take a step back and slow myself down considerably and this started to take a toll on my quality of life, and I started to become very frustrated.

Some days my leg would totally give way and I had to write that day off completely. It was hard; before I was just in a mental prison. But now I had to put up with a physical one as well as mental. I had taken for granted my physical fitness before.

This new existence, I was living on a cocktail of painkillers, TENS machine and visiting various chiropractors, physiotherapists and osteopaths to help my condition I had even had acupuncture, manipulation therapy and regularly saw a sports injury specialist.

At times these services were helpful but only for a short period and nothing provided permanent relief. It felt like an ongoing battle. If Jas used to humiliate me or hit me most of the time I just stayed quiet or ignored it as was trying to manage the pain and do the best I could each day. I was getting good at blocking him out now.

But at what cost? I completely blocked out my own emotions and found myself desperately unhappy and alone. It was building up on me, affecting my soul, quietly eroding my essence, as it became more and more normal to feel this downtrodden.

Jas and his family even said I would put on the pain, so I did not have to do house hold chores or go to the shop in the evening. I experienced constant invalidation and lack of support. I didn't even know what it felt like to be cared for and understood. I was just in my own little world at home. Jas didn't matter and his family didn't matter to me. I just wanted the most peaceful life that I could have at this point. I didn't really know what normal was, but this was my new kind of normal. I cherished the peaceful times. Even when we started living in our own flat Jas was expected to go to the shop, but I told him I could no longer go every evening due to my back pain. The resentment was growing all the time, it never gave up. The environment was never positive.

It was so deeply hurtful the things Jas would say about my back pain and deep down I always felt it was his fault for what he did that night. I would sometimes mention that to him, when he was in a good mood, but he would just say he was really sorry. Sorry was no good to me, as I was the one suffering each day.

I look back at those years and think it is crazy how much I suffered for nearly 8 years not even being able to walk for periods of the day! I still remember praying each night, asking God to help me so I could walk like before.

Looking Into My Medical Assessment: Depression

I did not know it at the time, but I look back at the medical assessment and I was certainly depressed. They had asked questions about how I had been over the week and it saddens me to read the following:

- Most of the time I felt totally lacking in energy and enthusiasm.
- I often felt terribly alone and isolated.
- Not at all did I feel I had someone to turn to for support when I needed it.
- Sometimes I felt able to cope when things go wrong.
- I was often troubled by aches, pains and other physical problems.
- I only occasionally had thoughts of hurting myself.
- I often felt tension and anxiety that prevented me doing important things.
- I only occasionally felt happy with the things I had done.
- I had been disturbed by unwanted thoughts and feelings often.
- Most of the time I felt like crying.
- I often felt panic and terror.
- Only occasionally was I able to do most things I needed to.

- Unwanted images and memories had been disturbing me often.

I am glad that I didn't hurt myself physically and I hadn't put my health at risk. However I know I often had suicidal thoughts which I had briefly shared with my mother, who told me that whatever happens I should never take my life, as my soul would not go home to God. I kept what she said in mind, but it never took away the feelings of wanting to end my life.

Eating Problems

I was vegetarian my whole life, but Jas would put meat in my food, and was extremely disrespectful. Jas just totally had no respect for my wishes. I never ever liked the taste of meat so I could pick out immediately if this had been placed into my food. I never placed any judgment on people who chose to eat meat however for me, I didn't like the taste, and also I felt like it impeded my spiritual development.

When I lived in London I had a balanced diet and certainly did not have any habits of eating junk food on a regular basis. However, while living with Jas's parents I started eating chocolates and crisps nearly every day especially if I had not had time to go home in between work and the shop to eat some dinner. The shop sold these junk food items.

I also stared eating alone in my bedroom, as I often did not like what was cooked in the house and this mainly meant eating junk items.

At times I would eat on my own and over fill myself. I would feel an instant relief while I was eating, but total disgust and sadness when I was too full. In essence I was binge and emotional eating. I gained weight, which initially I did not recognise and to be honest I did not really care at the time, as my interest in looking after my appearance had disappeared a long time ago.

Self-Worth, Confidence And Belonging

I had just become a shell of a person. The years of humiliation and derogatory remarks from Jas and his family had taken a toll on me. I had not an ounce of self-worth or confidence left in me. I also felt like I didn't belong anywhere and deep down so desperately wanted to be loved.

Over the years Jas and his family had just chipped away until there was nothing left. Jas had also impacted me financially and forced thousands and thousands of pounds out of me to fund their silly shop and pay off his credit cards. I just did not care anymore and would give the money as it was better than getting a beating. I even opened an ISA account and placed money in it so we would have some savings.

But deep down I was placing money away in a savings account; subconsciously as if I was preparing for my escape. But at the time I did not know that.

⁕ PROFESSIONAL INSIGHT

Health Problems Associated With Domestic Violence

Physical health problems

The WHO multi country study measures health status with a standardised questionnaire with the aim of assessing the extent to which physical and sexual violence were associated with adverse health outcomes. The survey focused on general health and disabling symptoms. Pooled analysis of all 15 sites found significant associations between lifetime experiences of domestic violence abuse and self-reported poor health and with specific health problems in the last 4 weeks; difficulty walking, difficulty with daily activities, pain, memory loss, dizziness and vaginal discharge. The increased risk varied by symptom, ranging from 50 to 80%. These significant associations were maintained in almost all of the sites. Between 19-55% of women who had ever been physically abused by their partner were ever injured.[79]

The first burden of disease analysis of domestic violence abuse was conducted in the Australian state of Victoria. It is reported that domestic violence abuse contributed to 8% to the total disease burden in women aged 15-44 years and 3% in all women. Most strikingly, domestic violence abuse was the leading contributor to death, liability and illness in women aged 15-44, being responsible for more of the disease burden than other diseases such as diabetes high blood pressure smoking and obesity. Poor mental health contributed 73% and substance misuse 22 % to the disease burden attributed to domestic violence abuse.[80]

Reproductive health problems have been the most extensively studied physical health consequence of domestic violence abuse. Low birth weight was found in women who reported physical, sexual or emotional abuse during pregnancy, compared with women who were not abused. Women who were abused were three times more likely to have kidney infections and were one and a half times more likely to deliver by caesarean section.[81]

Injuries are the most obvious manifestation of domestic violence abuse. Patients exposed to physical violence may present with injuries that vary from minor abrasions to life-threatening trauma. While there can be overlap between injuries resulting from domestic violence abuse and injuries from other causes, the former typically involve trauma to the head, face and neck. Multiple facial injuries are suggestive of domestic violence abuse rather than of other causes and those that are more specific for domestic violence abuse rather than of other causes and those that are more specific for domestic violence abuse include zygomatic complex fractures, orbital blow out fractures and perforated tympanic membrane. Musculoskeletal injuries are considered the second most common type of injuries, including sprains, fractures and dislocations.

Blunt force trauma to the forearms should raise suspicion of domestic violence abuse, as this can occur when trying to block being struck. The most severe consequence of domestic violence is death.[82]

It was found that all women subjected to physical violence also suffered from some form of psychological violence, with many also being sexually abused by their partners. These women also had been found to have a higher incidence and severity of anxiety and depressive symptoms, Post-Traumatic Stress Disorder, and a higher incidence of suicidal attempts.[82]

Binge Eating

Individuals with binge eating disorder engage in recurrent binge eating during which they eat an abnormally large amount of food over a short period of time. Unlike bulimia nervosa, patients with binge eating disorder do not compensate in any way after a binge episode. Binge episodes often occur in private, generally include foods of dense caloric content, and during the binge, the person feels he or she cannot control his or her eating. The actual cause of binge eating disorder is unknown. There is evidence to suggest that binge eating occurs during periods of stress. It may be used to reduce anxiety or alleviate depressive moods. Cognitive behavioural therapy is the most effective psychological treatment for binge eating disorder.[83] It has been shown to lead to decreases in binge eating disorder and associated problems (i.e. depression).

There is emerging recognition of the prevalence of eating disorders in already slim young Asian women who are striving for control, attractiveness and success in a patriarchal society.

Some studies have found lower levels of eating disorders in Asian women than in Caucasian women and assumed that their ethnic culture protects them against negative body image because it does not overvalue thinness. However, Asian women report less self-esteem and also dissatisfaction with racially defined body parts, such as eyes and facial features. Others identify higher prevalence of eating disorders amongst Asian women attributed to women's experiences of racism and sexism, that undermine their self-esteem and creates a poor body image.[84]

Asian Women And Suicide

Black and Asian women are considerably more at risk of attempting suicide, with prevalence ratios 1.6 times that of white women and 2.5 times that of Asian men. Young Asian women (under 30) are 2.5 times more likely to attempt suicide than white women and seven times more likely than Asian men. Domestic violence, including forced marriage, has been identified as a major factor in 49% of suicide attempts made by black women compared to 22% of suicide attempts by white women. Women experiencing domestic violence, who also have post-traumatic stress symptoms, are up to 15 times more likely.[85]

Medical records show up to 40% abused women in the Asian community attempt suicide while 25% women experiencing moderate to severe violence report regular suicidal thoughts, compared to 4% of women in general.

Highly dangerous suicide methods such as self-burning are more common amongst young Asian women, connected to the traditional practice of Hindu widows burning themselves on their husband's funeral pyre, known as "suttee".[86] Beliefs about death and spirituality may impact on suicidal behaviours. Muslims, for whom committing suicide is strictly forbidden, had relatively lower rates of suicide than Hindus, who believe in reincarnation or rebirth. However, a clinician should always talk with a patient about her personal beliefs about suicide rather than make assumptions on the basis of her religion.

In a West London study, Bhugra et al (1999) found that many of the Asian women attending a GP surgery who attempted suicide had made a previous attempt and previously had been diagnosed with medical or psychiatric illness. 31% wrote a suicide note before their attempt and

13% of them had written wills.[87]

Patel of Southall Black Sisters wrote about the reasons for the increased risk of suicide in Asian women,

"The challenge to religion and culture is not easy. The choice for many women who dare to break out of the very narrow confines of the roles prescribed by religion and culture is stark; either they remain within the parameters of permissible behaviour, or they transgress and risk becoming pariahs within their own community. Many women cannot even conceive of a life of isolation and loneliness, preferring instead to risk their health, sanity and even their lives. Suicide rates among Asian women between the ages of 16 and 35 are up to three times the national average."[88]

Stresses associated with suicide in Asian women include loneliness, rejection, marital conflicts, inter-generational conflicts, love failure and exam failure. Some were isolated by forced marriage and disenchanted with services based on past experiences or anticipated discrimination, while being under pressure to maintain family integrity whatever the personal costs.

Hope

When in difficulties, we look for a sense of hope in a way either through people, religion or spirituality (In Psychology/Counselling terminology this stage is called the Transpersonal level).[89] It's this hope that keeps us from falling to our perils. However the stages before this can be daunting.

No Hope, Lost Hope, and False Hope can not only leave you with a negative feeling, but can be debilitating and weakening.

Sewell (2009), talks about people from Black and Ethnic Minority (BME) backgrounds experience the impact of this lack of hopefulness because of:

1. Poor engagement and communication and therefore poorer empathy.
2. Negative stereotypes.

This sums up the understanding of the BME community and how we deal with problems. Discussing problems and issues is difficult especially for men, who are told to "man-up" and "be a man"; you find them burying their heads in the sand.

Similarly with DVA the victim has all hope taken away from them by the perpetrator. Hope is lost, which is quickly followed by self-confidence, self-belief and self-value.[90] Slowly the conditions of worth are stripped from the victim and with that hope is lost. As with time the abuse continues and false hope starts. False hope is an act or an assurance given with no actual meaning or aim to carry out the promise with a greater intent to defraud and deceive. The false hope fully dissolves any last shred of likelihood of anything positive happening, firmly placing the victim in a state of hopelessness, dejection and into a slump they can't get out off or too scared to get out of.

Self-Confidence

Bénabou & Tirole (2002) describe self-confidence as simply believing in yourself, the ability to be secure within yourself and your skills displays self-confidence. Whereas confidence in others is the ability to trust that they will complete a certain task within a framework.[91]

Johansson-Stenman, Olaf, and Peter Martinsson. (2006), take this a step further and use self-confidence in the form of self-confidence being projected and displayed outwards in areas such as cars, homes etc. This eludes that the outwards confidence that can be projected confidence or displaced confidence, means that you believe in objects or status to give you the confidence to be yourself. You can have an escaped victim of DVA who managed to change their life around and worked on becoming someone with "status" i.e. Doctor, Lawyer etc. They can start to mask their experiences of DVA which gives them low self-confidence, however giving that becoming a Doctor or Lawyer gives them a sense of self value that increases their confidence levels, they can use this to build their self-worth and self-esteem, and thus create their ideal self.[92]

CHAPTER 7
LEAVING

Dying Father

My estranged father had contacted me over 2 years ago as he was going in for a life threatening surgery, that he ended up surviving. I started to have some limited contact with him during this period and on a visit to London I went to see him in hospital. He was the only person that never asked me why I didn't have any children, and he didn't even ask to see my husband. He didn't even ask any questions about him. It's like he didn't want to know anything about him.

On that particular visit to the hospital I had taken my masters graduation photographs to show him.

As I crossed the ward, I saw him try to prop and straighten himself up on the pillow. I could tell he was in a lot of pain, but he put a smile on his face. His stoic, kind of emotionless smile, but that was father.

I sat on the edge of the bed and asked him how he was doing, and I leant in for a hug. As we embraced for a few seconds I pulled out my graduation photographs.

"I have something to show you father."

He took the photos into his hands and began beaming with joy. He kissed one of the photos,

"*You are going to change your whole pathway in life darling, I am so proud of you,*"

he paused and then went on to say,

"*It's very important to be happy dear you know.*"

I knew instantly that he realised I was not happy, and I knew he was also trying to tell me to leave Jas. We then went on to have an amazing conversation about his life and how regretful he was for doing what he did to my mother.

Every time I visited him he would ask if she could come along. I would always tell him that mother said she would visit when the time was right. I noticed the deep glint of sadness in his eyes as I said that.

My sister had taken the full time role of caring for father, and mother still supported him by making meals and sending them over.

In a way I felt sorry for this man; lying there defenseless; needing to rely on us all, when he tried to be so strong, so hard faced. Now all the regret, the years of repressed guilt was coming to the surface in his final days, and there was nothing he could do about it. That was the last time I would ever see my father alive.

I returned to our flat with something in me having changed, but I could not describe what it was. I was in the flat and Jas had left his phone behind. It kept ringing and eventually I picked it up. It was Terri, Jas's ex girlfriend,

"*When are you coming sweetheart, I'm missing you,*"

she said in this sickly sweet sensual tone.

I told Terri it was Jas's wife, and she was so apologetic and added that she has always wanted to meet me. I felt nothing about Jas having an affair. I was actually happy to be even more free of him. I agreed that I wanted to meet her, and we met the very next day in a coffee house near the shop.

The night before I was having a lot of thoughts. Thoughts about what she was going to be like, how she looked.

I was already seated with a chai latte when a bubbly blonde girl in her mid thirties approached me. I could see she was holding her belly.

Surely... not?

She ordered her drink and sat down. She began explaining how she fell pregnant with her long term boyfriend, but that she had always loved Jas, and she told me how hurt she was that he betrayed her for me. She said that they were planning a life together, and at the time she didn't know how she was going to move on, but she had tried to.

I really thought the baby was Jas's, and Terri commented that I looked disappointed when I heard that it wasn't.

"I thought that if you got back together, it would be easier for me to tell him I'm leaving."

Terri looked at me shocked, she didnt realise how much I wanted to get away from him.

I asked her if Jas had ever hit her, but she said he hadn't.

"We were together for 10 years when he met you. He left me high and dry. We were childhood sweethearts

and I was absolutely devastated. When he started to call me again I knew he was having problems with you, I didnt know what to do. I was just so relieved he wanted to be a part of my life again after cutting me off for so long. I was so bored with my partner Geoff. Eventually we struck up a friendship and he would come to my house a couple of nights a week after working at the shop, and spend a few hours with me."

I didn't know how to feel, it was mostly emptiness I felt, especially when it concerned Jas.

Terri went on to say that she couldn't believe he was hitting me and that his mothers had a very strange hold over him. We left the meeting on a good note, and I wished her well with her pregnancy and what ever she decided to do in the future.

Driving back to the house, I sighed a huge sigh of relief and looked up into the sky. The clouds were tinged with purple and blue tones and they looked beautiful and peaceful. For once, I felt completely at peace, and I knew I was going to go home and take charge of the whole situation and take back my life.

I walked through the door and Jas was sitting on the sofa watching sport. I matter of factly explained to him how I had picked up Terri's call and met her for coffee. He tried to say that nothing was going on between them, but I looked him squarely in the eyes and said,

"Jas, do you honestly think I care?"

I smiled truimphantly as I made my way to the bedroom.

That night I put my house in London up for sale, and started looking for somewhere to buy. Jas thought that we were going to have some time apart and reunite, but I told him the house would be put in my name. He had gone very quiet since I told him of Terri, and deep down he knew that I knew they were having an affair.

He had resigned to the situation, and there was a huge silence and emptiness in the house, but each day I woke up, I could feel like I was closer to my freedom.

About a month later my father was rushed back into the hospital, and this time we all knew that he was going to die. Mother went to visit him that night, she forgave him and my father closed his eyes to sleep.

The next morning she called me to tell me to get to the hospital as soon as I could because father was holding on by a thread.

Jas sat there and watched me rush about, trying to book a flight and pack a bag. My mother called me a few hours later and told me that father had passed.

At that moment, I dropped the phone and my face went cold. My knees fell to the ground and in such frustrated sadness, I punched the floor over and over again, screaming and screaming.

Jas saw this and walked out of the house. I was so angry. Angry that I couldn't be there for my father's last moments, angry about what he did to mother, upset that his face lit up when I showed him my masters graduation photos. A mixture of emotion was stirred up in me because of that man. But he was my father after all. I remember him pushing me on the swing in the park in Hammersmith we always used to go to when I was a child. I remember the kindness on his face and I would giggle and ask him to push me harder.

I was left in such as state that I barely made sense to British Airways while booking my flight. I had told them my father was dying and they told me that they reserve seats for these types of situations, so I booked my flight and went to the shop to ask Jas if he would drive me there.

The atmosphere was stormy in the car. Jas didn't say a single word to me, I was there alone in my grief, not a word of comfort or support. I remember feeling this cold heartedness, as he sat over from me in the driver's seat, the car so silent the indicators seemed deafening.

My head was spinning. I had so many questions. How was mother going to cope? How were the next few days going to go? We had so many people we had to contact and so many things to arrange it was going to be hugely stressful.

At the departures gate, I pulled my bag up the kerb and Jas didn't even get out to help me; as soon as I closed the door he was driving off.

The night before the funeral I stayed with my aunt, who didn't know me and Jas were seperated. So she had made up a bed for us. It was so awkward. What made it worse was that he tried to come onto me that night. But I firmly pushed him away and turned over.

On the day of the funeral Jas played the concerned husband, all caring and affectionate; but he was not fooling my immediate family. I told my mother I was in the middle of buying a house. All the paperwork had gone through, I just needed to pick up the keys when I returned from London.

She took me to one side of the funeral and said,

"Love, this has been a very dark day for me and the

family. But honestly I couldn't be hearing better news right now. I am so glad you are getting away from this monster. We will be able to sleep well at night once he is gone."

I glanced over at Jas who was looking a little lost talking to one of my uncles. Every passing day he was further and further away from me. I felt so sad about my father and would have liked to grieve in peace, but I knew things would get so much better for me once I left.

I returned a few weeks later after father's funeral, to be told by the solicitor that Jas had picked up the keys to my new house. I arrived at the new place to see Jas asking me to give us one more chance.

I literally wanted to laugh at this point. This guy was beyond crazy. He was so pathetic to me.

"I don't want to go back and live with my parents, please just give me six months to find a place, if you still want to end it after that time, then I will make a divorce simple."

I looked at his sad pathetic face. We both knew his time was completely up, but I agreed so he wouldn't be violent.

"You know how I feel Jas."

I walked off to the kitchen to make some food. The last few weeks had been so hard on our family. So many memories had been brought to the surface and it was taking a toll on me emotionally, plus the back pain, and there was extra pressure on at work due to some staff cutbacks. For once Jas was the least of my worries.

"This will all be over soon."

I muttered to myself as I sat down with my tea and toast.

Further Police Involvement

Jas and I were now leading very separate lives. I would still iron his shirts to avoid any disputes and cook some meals. A year had gone past and Jas was not leaving. He started to say he had a right to stay in the property. I gave him another few months and said after that I would seek legal advice.

By this point, I had made some friends at work, and was going out. On one work night out, I met a lovely guy called Andy, who was a friend of my work colleague.

The first night that I met him, I instinctively felt so protected and happy with this guy. His gentle nature and warm hearted eyes were such a comfort, such a blessing.

Andy knew of Jas, and said he only lived around the corner from me. That evening Andy and I walked home, and I told him what Jas was like to me in the past and how he would not leave the house. Andy was going to Barcelona for a week and said that I could take his spare key if anything happened and I needed to get away. I turned to him and gave him a huge hug with tears in my eyes.

Andy and his family became my life savers. Andy's mother would reassure me that they were my new family and would support me. This new found love and support helped me to gain the confidence to push for a solicitor. Andy even went with me to the appointment.

The legal proceedings were underway and this made Jas, a cowardly desperate man, start up the violence again, in last ditch attempts to try to batter me into submission so I didn't leave. In March and April 2004 he hit me again. My work colleague and Andy encouraged me to report the incidences, and I did, but I did not want to press charges as I just wanted him out of my life; I didn't want to make things worse. He kept threatening to clean me out financially and run off, and I was scared of this. My head was just above water as it was.

The second attack came after he had received a letter from the solicitor telling him about the court proceedings. He dragged me up against the office wall, banged my head against it, pulled my hair and squeezed my jaw so tightly that I couldn't breathe.

"You are killing me, you have ruined my life, look what you have done. All your plans have come true, you have ruined me! How dare you divorce me after all we have been through."

He kept on screaming as he bashed my head off the wall. I was in pain but I was completely numb to it mentally. I was waiting to get away so I could get help from Andy and his family. I was scared of Jas but nowhere near as much as before. His evil family weren't hovering around and I had Andy as backup.

Songs

I remember some key songs that helped me during the process of leaving Jas. These songs will always remain a part of me.

One song in particular; Tina Turner "What's Love Got to Do With It". Jas would always say he loved me so much and how he was so sorry. I would listen to Tina in my car and say to myself what has love got to do with it! Another track by Miss Dynamite, "You got to put him out" was my favourite too.

I played this song so regularly that the words started to merge with my soul. In particular the words such as "you've got to put him out, do take time to Love yourself, this time don't take him back, you can find real love with someone else, any real man agrees he ain't a man the first time he raised his hand". These true words gave me strength through this time.

No matter what Jas was saying to me about how much he loved me and I would play these songs to remind myself that what he was saying was totally dishonest.

I had a new perspective about our situation. I just wanted his behaviour to stop and be able to have a decent life again. This was getting into the seventh year married, and there was such a difference in how I felt. I would listen to songs like Toni Braxton's "Unbreak my heart" (say you'll love me again, undo the hurt that you caused, uncry these tears, I cried so many nights. I used to hold onto hope in the early years. Now I did not care at all, and I was ready to fight the social stigma.

It took me a long time and years and years of intense hurt to break my loyalty down to this point, but it made me much stronger as a person. I look back on these times and I am proud that I found the strenght on so many occasions to keep pushing forward in a hell that many would not be able to cope with. I survived.

Day Jas Left

We were in June 2004 now and as usual I heard the key turn in the lock. He was home. I was ironing his shirts, which I did to keep the peace. We were only communicating via written messages.

"Let's go out for lunch today sweetheart."

I prickled at the word.

"We are no longer together Jas, I do not want to go out with you."

He rushed towards me, got hold of my hair again, slapped me round the face, and punched my stomach several times. It never got easier, the physical violence and his brute force. He never held back, he hit me as if I were a full grown man. The amount of times I have had horrendously deep and painful bruises on my body are too many to count, the incidences kind of all blur into one. He stopped hitting me and told me that I made him violent and he walked out.

For the first time I had the courage to pick up the phone and call the police and told them what happened. I heard a knock at the door, it was a man, who looked really concerned.

"Oh my god love, you are so tiny. That scumbag was huge. The police are on the way. Can I make you a cuppa? The sugar will calm you down. I am so sorry".

About fifteen minutes afterwards, I was sitting on the couch with this man Derek, and a policeman knocked on the door. Derek let him in. As usual when these things happened to me, I would disassociate and blank out.

"I can see you have been hurt miss. This time you can press charges, you don't have to say anything. Your husband is at the police station. This kind gentleman saw the whole incident from the other side of the street as he was working on a gas problem, and he called the incident in before you did. He wants to provide a

supporting statement. Your husband tried to tell us that you had gone mad and had started to attack him. We are not believing his version of events at all. We are going to keep him in overnight in a cell, so please get your locks changed."

I thanked the both of them and immediately called Andy, who promised he would get his friend who was a locksmith round to sort all the locks out.

Andy came over that night and cradled me to sleep. I ended up crying in his arms like a small child. I was terrified that somehow Jas would be released and would turn up at the house. I was worried if he came back that him and Andy would get into a fight. I prayed and prayed to God that night in Andy's arms that this would be the very last time Jas attacked me.

Sadly, I was woken up by an early phone call from the police, saying that a member of the Asian community with some links to local MP's had come and they had to release Jas that evening, but they had advised him not to go anywhere near the house.

I got up and got dressed and as soon as the locksmith had finished, I went to the solicitor to gain an order so Jas couldn't come anywhere near the house. I still had Andy stay with me as I was scared that he would find a way to break into the house or do something to me, or get someone else to. Without hesitation he came to support me.

I was having nightmares and flashbacks of the incident, and I was constantly looking over my shoulder when I left the house, afraid that Jas would approach me and cause more trouble.

A couple of days after his arrest, Choti ma arranged via the police to come and pick his clothes up. When she turned up, I didn't say a word, and pointed to the black bags near the front door.

"He loves you so much my dear, why are you doing this? It is not like he stabbed you! When are you going to come back to the house dear?"

At that moment I wanted to scream at her and push her out of my house.

"I will never be coming back Choti ma, now please get out of here."

I will never forget her disgusting words.

✳ PROFESSIONAL INSIGHT

Approval

Marriage in any community is a big affair, but there is none bigger than the events the Asian community put on. In the UK an average British wedding can cost anything in the region of £23,000 on average whereas in the UK it's estimated (in a report by an Independent Newspaper) that an average Asian/Indian wedding would cost around £50,000 to £75,000 and generally speaking the price is on the increase.93

Lavish weddings are lovely events however when the demise comes, it comes with a barrage of hurt, damage, suffering and grief not to mention the cost of the lawyers/solicitors. Divorce is not an easy option even if you look at it from only a financial standpoint. This could be one of the reasons why victims of DVA stay in violent relationships.94

Why did the author need permission from her dying father to divorce her abusive husband? Was this guilt? Respect? Permission? Other reasons? The wedding was a huge event and must of cost a lot, especially when the grooms family asked for a huge dowry. There is added pressure and an expectation to make things work or continue until the bitter end.

This pressure could lead to a person feeling depressed, stressed and in a state of confusion. Was the act of the father passing away the catalyst that she needed? Was her father's final blessing enough for her to realise her self-worth and find her self-confidence?

Accepting that there have been failures is one thing but actually plucking up the courage to deal with it is something else. But we believe it was his permission that empowered Tara to become solid and steadfast and take control of her life.

Bereavement

Even uncomplicated grief encompasses a broad range of feelings and behaviours that are common after a loss. The characteristics of normal or acute grief are:[95]

- Somatic or bodily distress of some type.
- Preoccupation with the image of the deceased.
- Guilt relating to the deceased or circumstances of the death.
- Hostile reactions.
- The inability to function as one had done so before the loss.

Many of the normal grief behaviours such as sleep disturbances, appetite disturbances, absent minded behaviour, social withdrawal, searching and calling out, crying may seem like manifestations of depression. Freud in his early papers has pointed out that depression or 'melancholia' was a pathological form of grief and was very much like mourning except that it had a certain characteristic feature of its own - namely angry impulses toward the ambivalently "loved" person turned inward. Grief can quite often seem like depression and it is true that grief may even develop into it. The average grief process is around 12 months in length and a lot of support and healing is required to prevent a person from going into depression.[96]

Music

In this state of deep sadness, what a person listens to can help change their emotional state significantly. People use music as a form of guidance and/or therapy.

Research has found that the ability to recognise basic emotions in music, such as happiness and sadness, is a universal skill that does not always depend on previous exposure to the musical style (Fritz et al. 2009).

Depending on our internal emotional state we relate to the lyrics or music we hear. In upbeat songs we sing along to lyrics where can find strength and hope and in slower songs we tend to reflect upon our feelings more and focus on staying within that emotion to experience it fully.[97]

CHAPTER 8
JOURNEY HOME TO ME

Guilt

J as was gone and part of me was relieved but there was another part of me that was full of guilt.

I was aware that getting a divorce was not spiritually right. In my culture once you are married you make it work. I recall placing my two hands together and praying asking God to forgive me and in the same prayer saying to God that no one should be expected to stay in an abusive marriage.

The community did not help my feelings of guilt. One day I attended the Gurdwara and an older lady said to me that some husbands hit their wives and that is not a good enough reason to divorce them.

She also said God does not forgive people who get a divorce and that I would not have a place in heaven. When I said I was never coming back, I was told not to enter the house of God anymore.

Where I lived was largely a white community and my only access to my culture was the Gurdwara or at get together in their homes. I was totally disowned by the community and no longer welcome. I used to visit an Asian beautician and bless her she was happy to keep a relationship with me, but only in secret.

It was dispiriting to say the least but it was what I expected.

Jas wrote to my younger sister and here is a paragraph from that letter:

"I know that if Tara will listen to anyone, it is you, as she has a lot of respect for you. I'm not in a position to talk to your mother or family either and you are the only person I think I can possibly plead with, as I know that they are, including you are very hurt, angry and most probably very frightened for the wellbeing of Tara and are not in agreement in any chances of reconciliation. All I would like to say at this point, is that my feelings are in agreement with yours and your family, but I assure you that I will never do anything intentionally or otherwise to hurt or endanger your life or future, as she means more than the world to me. I only want the best for her and this has always been the case and has never changed since the day we met."

She sent me the letter and I read it several times. I couldnt believe that this was my life. It was so messed up and so fake in so many ways. I did not want to be a part of it anymore. I wanted to feel and create something real.

Jas would communicate with me via letters and state that God would never forgive me and in one letter said he wishes that in our next life he hoped we meet and spend our life together as husband and wife.

I suppose at the time guilt did play on my mind a lot and also a feeling of loss. It was a weird confused state to be in, because I lost a marriage but it wasn't a marriage at all really. It was years of hell that I was then free of. So it was surreal. I left that relationship feeling like I had effectively wasted seven years of my life, and when I left I felt like my life was just beginning.

But it did hit me really hard when I suffered racial abuse at work. When I needed the Indian community the most, they were not there. I was off work for a long time just after I left Jas, but I was successful in legal proceedings.

Andy And His Family

I will be forever grateful to Andy and his family, who supported me and helped me to not feel alone. My divorce took five long years and they were my shoulder to cry on when things got tough.

The years to follow were daunting and such a long drawn out process, considering we did not have any children and I was making no claim on any of his assets. It really affected my mental and physical health.

Jas's words still reverberated constantly in my mind "I am going to make you homeless" he said. He was claiming the house I brought without him was matrimonial property and wanted a share of it. But I recall calmly saying to Andy that I would rather be homeless than ever live with Jas again.

It was just typical of him to dish out low blows like that. It was really hard being on my own with no support from the community, but I had decided to make a new life and I had to remain steadfast and this was the final stance.

Health Back On Track

Intensive counselling started and this allowed me to reflect about my roles and identity in my culture and allowed me to explore the ways I was struggling to adapt in my new life.

In my marriage I wanted to be loved, appreciated and to feel a sense of belonging. The counselling helped me recognise that I had suffered from reactive and circumstantial depression in the past.

For my back and walking problems, I was referred to a holistic pain residential treatment clinic. I learnt how to manage my pain and slowly over time my self-belief and self-worth increased and the incidences where I couldn't walk diminished. I progressed to being able to walk without aids or having to wear a TENS machine or take strong painkillers.

This started my new journey into rebuilding Tara. I was symbolically walking into my new life and future.

My emotional eating is still a journey, but I promise myself to eat better, drink water and take regular light exercise. I no longer wish to disguise my past pain by filling myself up with comfort food. I want to live and get that smile back that I once had.

Loving Me

I went on a self-development journey reading books on healing the past, forums, and more recently attending various spiritual courses. This development started with the foundations to commence the process of forgiving Jas. I can forgive but can't forget. I never want to repeat the abuse cycle and be in such an appalling relationship again. But letting go and making peace with my past in itself has been beautiful and therapeutic. Peace was finally accomplished in a breakdown moment on a self-development event, which led to a break through moment and I had enough courage and bravery to be radically honest with myself. I courageously picked up the phone to Jas and said I truly forgave him for all he did to me. This was my closure and in this moment I felt true harmony and tranquility.

Jas by then had been to counselling himself and was able to truly reflect on our past. However, I took this time to recognise that Jas truly did not care for me as another human being. He did not state that he felt remorseful instead he complained to me that I was abusing him by having to listen to me going on about the past.

During our separation period Jas and I maintained a professional relationship. This was no real friendship, I felt that he was not genuine with me and he still could not see what he had done, but just purely for me to convince him to sign the divorce documents allowing me to move on.

It took a lot of back and forth for him to finally put pen to paper and sign the papers.

Even after the divorce I still encouraged Jas to seek help for himself as I never wanted another woman to experience what I had been through.

By travelling the journey of self-love, I forgave myself for allowing myself to stay in an abusive relationship for seven years and putting my own family through so much stress. My mother's health suffered as she was constantly worried for her daughter. We forget the people that love us, as we are going through so much, we forget that they fear for the safety of their loved ones.

One of my closest friends said, that before I was married, I was a beautiful confident woman, who was very successful, caring, kind, compassionate and very ambitious. Anything I put my mind to I would make it happen. I dressed well and looked after my appearance. I would enjoy my life, had amazing friends and experienced life to the full. I was always someone who was bubbly and had an amazing laugh, I was full of life.

The same friend said during my marriage and the period after I left Jas, I had no confidence, was walking on egg shells, no longer experiencing what life had to offer, like a walk in nature or seeing friends. I had no interest in my appearance or the clothes I wore. I'm became a timid mouse, when once I was a strong lion. The laughter from my mouth had gone and I no longer smiled.

I desperately wanted to find my laughter again, and my first smile came back in that moment the relationship was over forever.

I have now learnt to rekindle my love, respect and appreciation with myself and this makes this continuous journey more blissful and idyllic. I had lost Tara, the sparkle, the shine and the beauty. Nevertheless, the new rejuvenated Tara had been born steadfast, strong and brave. I had the vision to explore, expand and grow. Life was not about being frightened and anxious. Life was about being confident and in control.

Tara K. Today

I'm proud of my divorce label, I found the strength to deal with being disowned and of no longer having the presence and status of a husband, which is still so important in my culture.

Jas stated I was trash and came from a poor single parent family. Today I run successful businesses, which I would have never have done if I was with Jas. My work helps children and families impacted by domestic abuse. I am now helping other Tara's who were in similar situations to me.

Until the day I leave this beautiful earth I will remain committed to helping others impacted by domestic violence and abuse, by empowering them to rise above it and change themselves. I work with some of the most horrific circumstances.

My personal message to anymore suffering from domestic violence and abuse is,

"No one should treat you in a way that is abusive. Relationships are where we should feel safe, loved, cared for, nurtured and where we are encouraged and supported to be the best version of ourselves.

If I had never left I would not have the life I have today. I'm amongst family and friends that love me. My mother always said if I had not left, she always feared that one day she would be attending my funeral.

My message to society is that together we can reduce domestic violence if we remember that this person is someone's daughter or son. As many men are impacted by domestic violence. If you hear of it happening in your communities or families, lend a listening ear and do what you can to help. Do not turn a blind eye. As if it was not for the support of Andy and his family I may have left this world a long time ago.

My overall message is this: treat people with respect and care and as we are all human beings."

Future Plans

I have fully opened my heart to meeting my future partner, as for over a decade I never wanted to be in a long term relationship, because I was still scared of any future abuse.

However, by not opening myself up to a relationship, I would have never experienced the love, affection, care and unity that a true relationship will offer me. I will not allow my past to dictate my future for I deserve the happiness a loving relationship offers.

My final words to anyone in any type of abusive relationship,

"Know your worth, love yourself, have your own internal integrity and always remember a loving and caring relationship has no room for abuse. I know the journey to remove yourself from such a relationship will be hard. But if you stay, your internal light will find it hard to shine, and when you go your internal light will come back and you will come home to you."

✳ PROFESSIONAL INSIGHT

The Bigger Picture Of Domestic Violence Abuse

Warning Signs To Look Out For In Domestic Violence Abuse, And Cultural Barriers To Accessing Help

Divorce in the South Asian community was once a very taboo subject and it was hardly spoken of in the UK. This has changed drastically even in the past 10 years. It is not only happening here in the UK but in India divorce is raising significantly amongst the urban middle class in city areas. Dr Geetanjali Sharma, a marriage counsellor from Delhi says "There's been over 100% increase in divorce rates in the past five years alone." For any woman, the decision can be very hard but for an Asian woman it is much harder. The stigma of being divorced is still present and a woman's respect, status and honour (Izzat) relies on her marital status. The concept of honour (sharam) plays an important role in containing and policing many Asian women.[98]

Being married holds a certain reputation, respect and status. Women hold the honour of the family and their behaviour becomes the family honour.

The era of professional British Asians has begun. The trend in arranged marriages has dropped and the concept of meeting your own partners has grown. Now, British Asian marriages are a mix of love, arranged and even speed dating encounters. British Asian women have evolved to being financially and professionally secure, whilst British Asian men have thrived in all kinds of business and professional lifestyles and are no longer stereo-typed as corner-shop owners.

Young British Asian married couples are more commonly living independently from family. The notion of the extended family is eroding. Educated daughter-in-laws find it difficult to adapt to the traditional demands by in-laws and in return in-laws find it hard to understand new ways and accept change causing conflict and differences in opinion. These changes have impacted family life, breaking the nucleus that was once prominent in Asian households.[99]

Black and ethnic minority women are more likely than Caucasian women to face socio-economic risk factors for depression, including racial discrimination, lower educational and income levels, low status jobs or unemployment, poor health, larger family sizes, young children, physiological changes (e.g. around childbirth) isolation and immigration issues. Most of these are increased by domestic violence.[100] In contrast, factors that protect mental health include experiences of positive parenting, good family support, good social networks and good housing. Most of these are disrupted by domestic violence. Depression in South Asian women is associated with difficulties such as feeling trapped. Coercive control behaviours may manifest as:

- Isolation from friends, family and other support networks.
- Limited access to money.
- Surveillance of everyday tasks such as grocery shopping.
- Intercepting mail, phone calls and text messages.
- Threats to harm or kill children.

Harassment and stalking may also form a part of a general pattern of coercion and control, although these behaviours are sometimes regarded as distinct from one another. Common stalking behaviours include unwanted communication (phone calls, text messages or emails), being followed on the street, contacted at work or home, unwelcome visits or gifts, threats, damage to property, violence and gaining information about the victim under false pretenses.[101]

By now, it is clear to say that victims of DVA often leave their abusive partners. Those who stay, hoping the violence and emotional/psychological will stop, are usually disappointed. Once women realise that the relationship will not change, they eventually begin the process of escape.

Research on 60 Asian women found: 55% experienced domestic abuse: 46 from their husbands and 10 also from their mother-in-law. All women with experience of domestic abuse identified impacts on their mental health, particularly depression, anxiety and suicidal thoughts. 73% were unaware of services available to support Asian women.[102]

Health professionals are in a unique position to help Asian women who are experiencing domestic violence as they will come into contact with them at some point through the services they provide. By providing a safe environment in which Asian women feel they can disclose, information and support can be made available which could potentially save their lives and certainly make a difference to them and their children.

Health professionals are often a first point of contact for women and they deal with the after effects of domestic abuse on an everyday basis. Women who have experienced abuse use health services frequently and require wide-ranging medical services. They are likely to be admitted to hospital more often than non-abused women and are issued more prescriptions.[103]

A woman's health records can be crucial in legal proceedings. They can help a woman access her housing and welfare rights as well as influence the outcome of criminal and civil cases and immigration decisions. Time and again survivors of domestic abuse have said they wish somebody had asked them if they were experiencing problems in their personal relationships.104   Someone to talk about their attempts at suicide and self-harm, in the context of women's reluctance to disclose distress within their own community, because of a perceived stigma attached to any form of mental distress.   They need someone to validate a women's experience; someone to make the link between domestic violence and poor health.

Health professionals keep detailed, accurate records (safely) and confidentially. They will also refer to appropriate services, provide resources (e.g. a telephone, interpreter, computer) for her to access support.105 They will also provide first language services where possible.

General Practitioners surgeries can improve on having material available in the surgery in appropriate languages detailing relevant local resources for example, refuges for Asian women and to use advocates when these are available.

In this story, Tara talks about how with **support and hope** from Andy and her own family and friends allowed her to once again find **self-love, worth and confidence**. She **healed and forgave** the people that hurt her to become the hugely successful business woman she is today. She feels an immense amount of **gratitude** and wishes to continue empowering other victims of Domestic Violence and Abuse.

Studies have shown that social isolation and loneliness are associated with a higher risk of poor mental health and poor cardiovascular health, as well as other health problems.

Other studies have demonstrated the benefit of a network of social support, including the following: Improving the ability to cope with stressful situations, alleviating the effects of emotional distress, promoting lifelong good mental health, enhancing self-esteem, lowering cardiovascular risks, such as lowering blood pressure, promoting healthy lifestyle behaviours and encouraging adherence to any medical or treatment plans.[106]

Having support is the main backbone of building up self-worth again.[107] It teaches us how to live in hope, heal, forgive and love ourselves enough so that we can also love others again.

Psychology today highlight that there are seven scientifically proven benefits of gratitude;

Gratitude opens the door to more relationships; and it improves physical health and improves psychological health. Gratitude enhances empathy and reduces aggression, increases mental strength and improves self-esteem.[108] Grateful people also sleep better! [109]

Safety planning: What should a safety plan cover?[110]

A victim is always the best judge of risk and her own expert on safety. You might ask her to consider the following (but not advise her)

Safety in the relationship:

- Places in the house or outside to avoid.
- People to turn to for help or to inform about the danger.
- Asking neighbours to call 999 if they hear sounds of disturbance.
- Places to hide important phone numbers, such as helpline numbers.
- How to keep the children safe when abuse starts.
- Teaching the children to get help, perhaps by dialing 999.

- Keeping important documents in one place so that they can be taken in a hurry.
- Letting you record the abuse in case it can be of help in the future.

Leaving in an emergency

- Packing an emergency bag and hiding it in a safe place.
- Plans for who to call and where to go (such as a domestic violence refuge).
- Things to remember to take: documents, medication, keys.
- Access to a phone.
- Access to money or credit/debit cards that a woman may have put aside.
- Plans for transport.
- Plans for taking clothes, toiletries and toys for the children.
- Taking any proof of the abuse, such as photos, notes or names of witnesses.

Safety when a relationship is over

- Contact details for professionals who can advise or give vital support.
- Changing landline and mobile phone numbers.
- How to keep her location secret from her abusers (e.g. not going to same temple).
- Applying for a non-molestation order.
- Talking to children about the importance of staying safe.
- Asking an employer for help with safety while at work.

Building a long-term future

- Sessions with counsellors who communicate in the first language.
- Access to community based services.
- Social support including new groups of friends.
- Educational or work opportunities to secure financial independence.
- Help with budgeting and understanding social systems.
- Follow up from known and trusted professionals.
- Re-establishing contact with any safe members of the family.

ABOUT THE AUTHORS

Tara K.

Tara is a qualified Social Worker, who holds an MSc in Advanced Professional Studies and has further qualifications in Practice Education, Management, Leadership and Self-Development.

In her professional roles she has worked in mental health, child care, child protection, adoption, adults with learning disabilities and in the field of regulating and inspecting for care services. She has developed practice to promote equality and diversity in society.

She is a female entrepreneur who is a Director of a successful fostering agency in London making a difference to vulnerable children.

Tara's UK and international philanthropy work, is widespread into many areas such as human trafficking, honour based crime, forced marriages , mental health and domestic violence impacting both men and women. She has supported various orphanages internationally to provide care for young children.

She is a carer to her mother and a co-parent to three beautiful girls.

Tara is a survivor of horrific domestic violence abuse from

her former husband, and now through her book and motivational speaking she is empowering individuals, to live a life where they are loved, appreciated and respected.

The reason she wrote this book, is that she understands that when suffering from domestic violence it is easier said than done to leave the partner. Domestic abuse can affect the mind, body and soul, and indeed it distorts the identity of self. The aim of writing this book is to encourage other victims to be empowered when making the decision to leave.

Domestic violence impacts people from all backgrounds. The power of how domestic violence takes over your life can impact anyone, no matter what their cultural background, professional status or socio - economic background.

She wrote this book with two leading professionals, so not only was it her personal story told, but professional insights were included to enable people to leave their abusive partners and never return.

Finally, she believes that each one of us deserves a relationship where we are respected, loved, appreciated, supported and enhanced and where abuse of any form has no home. For home is where you should feel the safest and have a true sense of belonging.

Dr. Ravjot Kaur

Dr Ravjot Kaur is the Managing Director at *Seek Sense* (www.seeksense.co) and is an Associate Specialist in Psychiatry. As well as her degree in Medicine, she has post degree qualifications in - NLP, Timeline Therapy, CBT, Diploma in DBT, Hypnotherapy and Body language & Micro-expression Readings. Her ability at building a close rapport, listening and intuitively guiding her clients through their difficult time is her gift. She is particularly focused on building the bridge to understanding mental illnesses in a growing multicultural society.

Dr Kaur has worked in a broad range of General Medicine and Surgery including - ENT, Ophthalmology, Palliative Care and Elderly Care. She is a member of the Royal College of Psychiatrists and within Psychiatry she has experience in General Adult, CAMHS, Forensic, Liaison, Old Age Psychiatry and Personality Disorders all in Central and North West London. She has worked both within the NHS and Private Care establishments.

She is a producer of *Mental Health Matters* on Sangat TV Sky channel 755, and also appeared on BBC Two's *Victoria Derbyshire* television show along with Dr Michael Mosley discussing the use of placebos in pain management.

Harpal S. Chatwal

Harpal Singh Chatwal (MSc, BSc (Hons), MBACP (Accred)) is head of Domestic Abuse Service in South West London, a mental health campaigner, award winning broadcaster and accredited counsellor. His empathy, humanity and overriding concern for his clients' wellbeing have roots deep within his Sikh faith. His gentle approach has helped the most vulnerable clients find their own voice and inner courage to cope in the face of what to many would feel like insurmountable problems.

Harpal is a pioneer, firstly as one of the very few Asian and Sikh men who have chosen psychotherapy as their profession and in working with men who use violence as a method of control over their partners. He is a role model for both communities. His television series 'Mental Health Matters' has for the first time brought culture sensitive topics around mental health to a worldwide Asian audience.

To survive abuse and domestic violence takes the highest form of courage. Each survivor's story is unique, their needs diverse and their pain raw. This book is an essential insight into one survivor's story and the support that is available on their journey to safety.

REFERENCES

1. https://www.britannica.com/topic/violence Site accessed January 2019

2. Crowe, M. & Wylie, K., 2017. Overcoming relationship problems. 2nd ed. London: Constable and Robinson Ltd.

3. Office National Statistics, 2018. New definition of domestic violence. [Online]
Available at: https://www.gov.uk/government/news/new-definition-of-domestic-violence
[Accessed 13 January 2019].

4. World Health Organisation, 'World Report on Violence and Health', ed. By Krug, Etienne G., et al., Geneva, 2002; Moffitt, Terrie E., and Avshalom Caspi, 'Findings About Partner Violence from the Dunedin Multi-Disciplinary Health and Development Study', Research in Brief, National Institute of Justice, Washington DC, July 1999; Kishor, S., and Johnson, K., 'Profiling Domestic Violence – A Multi-Country Study', Calverton MD: ORC Macro, 2004; Population Information Program, 'Ending Violence Against Women', Population Reports, Series L, Number 11, 1999; Victoria Department of Human Health Services, 'The Health Costs of Violence, Measuring the Burden of Disease Caused by Intimate Partner Violence', Victoria, 2004.

5. https://www.cji.edu/site/assets/files/1921/domestic_abuse_report.pdf Site accessed in December 2018

6. The UK Government, 1998. Human Rights Act 1998. [Online] Available at:
http://www.legislation.gov.uk/ukpga/1998/42/contents
[Accessed 13 January 2019].

7. http://www.healthtalk.org/peoples-experiences/domestic-violence-abuse/womens-experiences-domestic-violence-and-abuse/getting-help-doctors-and-other-health-professionals-domestic-violence-and-abuse accessed January 2019

8. Howarth, E. & Feder, G., 2013. Prevalance and physical health impact of domestic violence. In: D. Howard, G. Fefer & R. Angew-Davies, eds. Domestic Violence & Mental Health. London: Bell & Bain Limited, pp. 1-17.

9. Nicolaides, C & Paranjape, A (2009) Defining Intimate partner violence. Pp 39-52. Oxford University Press

10. Mills, Linda G. Violent Partners: A Breakthrough Plan for Ending the Cycle of Abuse (2008)

11. Boy, A & Salihu, H.Mm (2004) Intimate partner Violence and birth outcomes; a systemic review. International Journal of Fertility, 49, 159-163.

12. Hague, G. & Malos, E., 1993. Domestic Violence - Action For Change. London: New Clarion Press.

13. Follingstad, D R., Rutledge, L. L., Berg, B. J., et al (1990) The role of emotional abuse in physically abusive relationships. Journal of Family Violence, 5, 107-120.

14. Schnurr MP, Mahatmya D, Basche RA III. (2013). The role of dominance, cyber aggression perpetration, and gender on emerging adults' perpetration of intimate partner violence. Psychol Violence. 3, 70–83.

15. https://nnedv.org/content/about-financial-abuse Site accessed in January 2019

16. https://bmcpsychiatry.biomedcentral.com/articles/10.1186/s12888-018-1890-9 Site accessed in January 2019

17. Sadock, B. J., Sadock, V. A. & Ruiz, P., 2017. Concise Textbook of Clinical Psychiatry. 4th ed. London: Wolters Kluwer.

18. Brockner, J. & Siegel, P., 1996. Understanding the Interaction Between Procedural and Distributive Justice: the Role of Trust. In: R. Kramer & T. Tyler, eds. Trust in Organisations. Thousand Oaks: CA: Sage, pp. 390-413.

19. Homans, G., 1961. Social Behaviour: Its Elementary Forms. New York: Harcourt Brace Jovanovich.

20. Metha, A. T., Kinnier, R. T. & McWhirter, E. H., 1989. A pilot study on the regrets and priorities of women. Psychology of Women Quarterly, Issue 13, pp. 167-174.

21. Lecci, L., Okun, M. A. & Karoly, P., 1994. Life regrets and current goals as predictors of psychological adjustment. Journal of Personality and Social Psychology, 66(2), pp. 731-741.

22. Atkins, B., 2013. Personal safety for social workers and health professional. Northwich: Critical Publishing Ltd.

23. Golightley, M., 2011. Social Work and Mental Health. 4th ed. London: SAGE Publications Ltd.

24. The General Social Care Council (GSCC) Codes of Practice for Employers of Social Care Workers www.gscc.org.uk

25. Skills for Care www.skillsforcare.org.uk. Good Practice Guide for employers in healthcare in relation to their safety

26. Guru, S (1986) ' An Asian women refuge.' In S Ahmed,J. Cheetham and J. Small (eds) Social work with Black Children and their families. London; B.T. Batsford.

27. Ahmed, S (1986) ' Cultural racism in work with Asian women and girls.' In S. Ahmed, J. Cheetham and J. Small (eds) Social Work with Black Children and their Families. London; B.T. Batsford.

28. Brah, A. And Minas, R. (1985) 'Structural racism or cultural difference; Schooling for Asian girls.'

29. Anwar, M. (1998) 'Between Cultures. Continuity and Change in the Lives of Young Asians. London and New York; Routledge.

30. Bhopal, K (1996) Gender, 'Race" and Patriarchy- A Study of South Asian Women. Aldershot; Ashgate.

31. Imam, U. F. (1999) ' Youth workers as mediators and interpreters- working with black young people.' In S. Banks (ed) Ethical Issues in Youth Work. London; Routledge.

32. Modood, T,. Beishon, S and Virdee, S (1994) Changing Ethnic Identities. London; PSI

33. Kemshall, H. Pritchard, J. (1999) Good Practice in Working with Violence. London. Jessica Kingsley Publishers.

34. Mama, A (1988) The Hidden Struggle; Statutory and Voluntary Sector Responses to Violence Against Black Women. London; LRHU/ Runnymede Trust.

35. Afshar, H. (1989) Three Generations of Women in Bradford. Paper presented at the Conference of Socialist Economists.

36. Bhachu, P. (1988) ' Home and work; Sikh women in Britain.' In S. Westwood and P. Bhachu (eds) `enterprising Women; Ethnicity, Economy and Gender Relations. London and New York; Routledge.

37. Brah, A. (1992) 'Women of South Asian origin in Britain.' In P. Braham, A. Rattansi and R. Skellington (eds) London:Sage/OU

38. Parmar, P. (1982) 'Gender, race and class- Asian women in resistance.' In Centre for Contemporary Studies The Empire Strikes Back. London; Hutchinson.

39. Ahmed, S., Waller, G. And Verduyn, C. (1994) 'Eating attitudes among South Asian schoolgirls. The role of perceived parental control.' International Journal of Eating Disorders, 15, 1, 91-97.

40. Raleigh, S. (1996) ' Suicide patterns and trends in people of Indian sub-continent and Caribbean origin in `England and Wales.' Ethnicity and Health 1, 1, 55-63.

41. www.equation.org.uk Asian Women, Domestic Violence and Mental Health, Barriers to accessing help.pdf 2012

42. Goffman, E., 1969. The Presentation of Self in Everyday Life. London: Allen Lane The Penguin Press.

43. Mikko, K. & McGookin, D., 207. Investigating User Generated Presentations of Self in. International Journal of Human-Computer Studies, 104(1), pp. 1-15.

44. Kohut, H., 1971. The Analysis of Self. Madison, CT: International Universities Press.

45. Patton, M. J. & Meara, N. M., 1992. Psychoanalytic Counseling. Chichester: Wiley.

46. Argyle, M., 2008. Social encounters: Contributions to social interaction. New York: Aldine Transaction.

47. Novaco, R W. (1998). Anger Workshop. Dublin; Trinity College Press

48. Kelly, G. A. (1970). Behaviour as an experiment. In D Bannister (ed), Perspectives in. Personal Construct Theory. London; Academic Press.

49. Russell, M. (1995).. Confronting Abusive Beliefs: Group Treatment for Abusive Men. Thousand Oaks, CA: Sage.

50. Kopper, B.A & Epperson, D. L. (1991). Women and anger. Psychology of Women Quarterly, 15 (1), 7-14

51. Haynes, S G., Levine, S., Scotch, N., Feinleib, M. & Kannel, W.B. (1978). The relationship of psychosocial factors to coronary heart disease in the Framingham study: I. Methods and risk factors. American Journal of Epidemiology, 107, 362-383

52. Cummins, P. (2006) Working with Anger- a constructive approach. Wiley & Sons

53. Golding, M. J. (1999) Intimate partner violence as a risk factor for mental disorders; a meta analysis. Journal of Family Violence, 156-163

54. Trevillion, K., Oram, S., Feder, G., et al (2012) Experiences of domestic violence and mental disorders; a systematic review and meta analysis.

55. Howard, L. M. Feder, G., Agnew- Davies, R. Domestic Violence and Mental Health.

56. https://www.ncbi.nlm.nih.gov/pubmed/24524716 Somatisation in Asians Site accessed in January 2019

57. https://icd.who.int/browse10/2014/en#/F45.3 Somatic symptoms Site accessed January 2019

58. https://www.healthline.com/health/hypothyroidism/stress-and-your-thyroid Site accessed January 2019

59. https://www.ons.gov.uk/peoplepopulationandcommunity/birthsdeathsandmarriages/deaths/datasets/suicideinenglandandwales. Suicide rates 2018

60. https://www.nice.org.uk/advice/ktt8/chapter/evidence-context. NICE GUIDELINES site accessed Jan 2019

61. https://www.nhs.uk/common-health-questions/medicines/how-should-antidepressants-be-discontinued Site accessed January 2019

62. https://www.health.harvard.edu/diseases-and-conditions/going-off-antidepressants Site accessed January 2019

63. https://www.marriage.com/advice/counseling/benefits-of-marriage-counseling-before-divorce Site accessed in January 2019

64. https://www.ons.gov.uk/peoplepopulationandcommunity/crimeandjustice/articles/domesticabusefindingsfromthecrimesurveyforenglandandwales/yearendingmarch2018 Site accessed January 2019

65. https://www.womenshealth.gov/relationships-and-safety/effects-violence-against-women Site accessed February 2019

66. Gill, A. (2004) Voicing the Silent Fear: South Asian Women's Experiences of Domestic Violence.

67. http://www.equation.org.uk/wp-content/uploads/2016/02/EQ-LIB-036.pdf
Coping with mental health problems in Asian women Section 4 page 18

68. http://www.equation.org.uk/wp content/uploads/2016/02/EQ-LIB-036.pdf
Section 5.2 Anxiety page 20

69. Gilbert, P, Bhundia, R, Mitra, R et al (2007) Cultural differences in shame-focused attitudes towards mental health problems in Asian and Non-Asian student women. Mental Health, Religion and Culture, 10(2): 127-141

70. Gupta, S (1990). The mental health of Asians in Britain. Letter. British Medical Journal, 301240

71. White, G. E. & Mullen, P. E., 1989. Jealousy: Theory, Research and Clinical Strategies. Guildford: New York Press.

72. Meloy, J. R., 1992. Violent Attachments. New Jersey: Aronson.

73. Karban, K 2011. Social Work and Mental Health. Polity Press

74. Sadock, B. J., V. A., Ruiz, P. Kaplan & Saocks Concise Textbook of Clinical Psychiatry. Kleptomania pg 256

75. https://www.researchgate.net/publication/228426621 Stranger Danger Explaining Women%27s Fear of Crime site accessed January 2019

76. https://www.nidirect.gov.uk/articles/police-procedures site accessed February 2019

77. https://www.met.police.uk/advice/advice-and-information/daa/domestic-abuse/af/clares-law/
site accessed in Feb 2019

78. https://www.gov.uk/government/news/government-publishes-landmark-domestic-abuse-bill
site accessed in Feb 2019

79. Ellsberg, M., Jansen, H. A., Heise, L., et al (2008) Intimate partner violence and women's physical and mental health in the WHO multi- country study on women's health and domestic violence; an observational study. Lancet, 371, 1165-1172

80. Vos, T., Atbury, J., Piers, L. S., et al (2006) Measuring the impact of intimate partner violence on the health of women in Victoria, Australia. Bulletin of the World Health Organisation, 84, 739-744

81. Cambell, J. C., Woods, A.B.., Laughon Choauf, K., et al (2000) Reproductive health consequences of intimate partner violence: a nursing research review. Clinical Nursing Research, 9, 217-239

82. Povey, D. (ed.) (2004) Crime in England and Wales 2002/3; Supplementary Volume 1- Homicide and Gun Crime. Home Office Statistical Bulletin

83. Fairburn, Dr C.G., Overcoming Binge Eating, The Guilford Press

84. Department of Health (2002) Women's Mental Health; into the Mainstream. Strategic Development of Mental Health Care for Women London: Department of Health Publications (ref 29433/Womens mental health)

85. Lee, S. And Katzman, M. A, (2002) Cross Cultural Perspectives on Eating Disorders in D. Fairburn and K.D. Brownell (eds) Eating Disorders and obesity; a comprehensive handbook (2nd Edition) Guilford PRess, P 260-292

86. Raleigh & Balarajan (1992) Suicide and self-burning among Indians and West Indians in England and Wales. British Journal of Psychiatry , 161; 365-8

87. Bhugra, D., Baldwin, D.S., Desai, M. & Jacob, K.S. (1999b). Attempted suicide in West London. 11. Rates across ethnic communities. Psychological Medicine, 29, 1131-1139

88. Patel. P, (2000). Domestic violence campaigns and alliances across the divisions of race, gender and class. In J. Hanmer & C Itzin (eds). Home truths about domestic violence. Feminist influences on policy and practice. A reader, p. 167-184. London; Routedge

89. Clarkson, P., 2002. The therapeutic relationship. 2nd ed. London: Whurr.

90. Nuttall, J., 2008. The integrative attitude–a personal journey. European Journal of Psychotherapy & Counselling, 10(1), pp. 19-38.

91. Benabou , R. & Tirole, J., 2002. Self Confidence and Personal Motivation. Quarterly Journal of Economics, 117(3), p. 871–915.

92. Johansson-Stenman, O. & Martinsson, P., 2006. Honestly, Why Are You Driving a BMW. Journal of Economic Behaviour and Organisation, 60(2), pp. 129-46.

93. https://eventcentre.co.uk/much-asian-wedding-cost site accessed in January 2019

94. Shaddock, D., 2000. Contexts and Connections: An Intersubjective Approach to Couples Therapy. New York: Basic Book.

95. Worden, J. W. Grief Counselling and Grief Therapy. Brunner-Routledge

96. https://www.psychologytoday.com/gb/blog/thriving-in-the-face-trauma/200910/grief-doesnt-come-in-stages-and-its-not-the-same-every

97. Fritz, T. H., Schmude, P., Jentschke, S., Friederici, A. D., and Koelsch, S. (2013c). From understanding to appreciating music cross-culturally. *PLoS One* 8:e72500. doi: 10.1371/journal.pone.0072500

98. https://www.bbc.co.uk/news/world-south-asia-12094360 site accessed January 2019

99. https://www.desiblitz.com/content/life-after-marriage-for-british-asians site accessed January 2019

100. Gill, A (2005). Against my will – violence, suicide and honour. Safe – the Domestic Abuse Quarterly www.womensaid.org.uk

101. Traumatic distress among support- seeking female victims of stalking. American Journal of Psychiatry, 158, 795-798

102. Fenton, S & Karlsson, S (2002). Explaining their mental distress: narratives of cause. In W. O'Connor (ed) Ethnic differences in the context and experience of psychiatric illness: qualitative study (EDCEPI) London: Department of Health

103. Department of Health (2005) Responding to Domestic Abuse: A Handbook for Health Professionals, p.26

104. Wong, J.M., Huang, V.Y., Chan, SS et al (2003) S. OS: Shame, Obligation and Survival: Asian Americans and Domestic Violence. In L. Zhan (ed). Asian Americans: Vulnerable Populations, Model Interventions and Clarifying Agendas, ch. 7, p. 135-170, Jones and Bartlett Publishers

105. Chew-Graham , C. et al., 2002. South Asian women, psychological distress and self-harm: lessons for primary care trusts. 5(10), pp. 339-47.

106. http://www.theworldcounts.com/life/potentials/social-support-is-vital-to-your-health Site accessed January 2019

107. https://www.ncbi.nlm.nih.gov/pubmed/10835830 Effects of social support and self-esteem on depressive symptoms in Japanese middle-aged and elderly people. Site accessed January 2019

108. https://www.psychologytoday.com/gb/blog/what-mentally-strong-people-dont-do/201504/7-scientifically-proven-benefits-gratitude Site accessed in January 2019

109. https://www.psychologytoday.com/gb/blog/minding-the-body/201111/how-gratitude-helps-you-sleep-night Site accessed in January 2019

110. Safety cover adapted from Department of Health (2005) Responding to Domestic Abuse

23497375R00104

Printed in Great Britain
by Amazon